T0196030

TRAVEL FOR
FREE!

Earning Incentive Travel
with Your Business

JILL STEVENS

Foreword by Steve Wiltshire

BALBOA.PRESS
A DIVISION OF HAY HOUSE

Balboa Press books may be ordered through booksellers or by contacting:

Balboa Press
A Division of Hay House
1663 Liberty Drive
Bloomington, IN 47403
www.balboapress.com
844-682-1282

Because of the dynamic nature of the Internet, any web addresses or links contained in this book may have changed since publication and may no longer be valid. The views expressed in this work are solely those of the author and do not necessarily reflect the views of the publisher, and the publisher hereby disclaims any responsibility for them.

The author of this book does not dispense medical advice or prescribe the use of any technique as a form of treatment for physical, emotional, or medical problems without the advice of a physician, either directly or indirectly. The intent of the author is only to offer information of a general nature to help you in your quest for emotional and spiritual well-being. In the event you use any of the information in this book for yourself, which is your constitutional right, the author and the publisher assume no responsibility for your actions.

Any people depicted in stock imagery provided by Getty Images are models, and such images are being used for illustrative purposes only. Certain stock imagery © Getty Images.

The ESV® Bible (The Holy Bible, English Standard Version®). ESV® Text Edition: 2016. Copyright © 2001 by Crossway, a publishing ministry of Good News Publishers. The ESV® text has been reproduced in cooperation with and by permission of Good News Publishers. Unauthorized reproduction of this publication is prohibited. All rights reserved.

Scripture taken from the New King James Version®. Copyright © 1982 by Thomas Nelson. Used by permission. All rights reserved.

THE HOLY BIBLE, NEW INTERNATIONAL VERSION®, NIV® Copyright © 1973, 1978, 1984, 2011 by Biblica, Inc.® Used by permission. All rights reserved worldwide.

Print information available on the last page.

ISBN: 978-1-9822-5567-1 (sc)
ISBN: 978-1-9822-5569-5 (hc)
ISBN: 978-1-9822-5568-8 (e)

Library of Congress Control Number: 2020918687

Balboa Press rev. date: 02/10/2021

DEDICATION

To Jessica Fletcher and Angela Lansbury who brought her to life, for inspiring me that it is never too late to begin your writing career. I'm only just getting started. Thank you!

CONTENTS

FOREWORD

Life offers itself to us in an endless number of ways through inspiration! Jill Stevens was a conduit for inspiration to write a book unlike any other that has ever been written in the Direct Sales & Network Marketing World. *"Travel For Free"* will evoke your vision to strive to live your ideal life style, for a destination where you will celebrate your achievements and pay it forward by bringing others on the journey with you! The truth is most people are living a life of status quo instead of a life of vitality, fulfillment and abundance. Most only accept a tiny fraction of the exciting possibilities around them! Jill is a VISIONARY and for years has purposely guided others to see that *'There is another way!'* I know this because I have had the honor to be her Coach! Jill's mission is to empower humans to live a life of vitality and one that takes their breath away! She is constantly expressing her deep appreciation for finding our industry, or better said, attracting the industry into her life and feels a deep conviction to guide others to attract what they want! Jill will teach you how to attract what you want in your life through a faith, thinking, and belief mindset.

"Travel For Free" is a story about a destination of discovering your ideal life, evoking the greatest version of yourself and learning how to build a successful business in Direct Sales. Oh yeah and celebrating at a destination somewhere around the world on an all-expense paid trip through your Company. Whether you are exploring Direct Sales or currently with a Direct Sales or Network Marketing Company, Jill's book will amplify your vision and teach you fundamental practices that have brought success to numerous Direct Sellers. If you are a leader, this book is the perfect tool to inspire and train your team to achieve as well. You'll lose track of time through the animated stories in this book that will inspire you to earn your Company's next incentive trip! What might change in your life if you allow inspiration to guide you? Jill, you remind us all that inspiration is real and when we SAY YES, it guides us True North!

Steve Wiltshire, Direct Sales Author, Success Trainer & Life Coach

INTRODUCTION

TRAVELING – IT LEAVES YOU
SPEECHLESS, THEN TURNS YOU INTO
A STORYTELLER. ~ IBN BATTUTA

At one point during my 20-plus year direct sales journey, I listened to a taped program that was supposed to tell me exactly how to take cold leads and turn them into "hot prospects". I enjoyed the program, but at the end of the presentation, I still didn't know how to turn the leads into hot prospects. I was scratching my head. Had I missed something? I listened again, thinking the secret must have been in there somewhere. It wasn't. That was exactly how I did not want my readers to feel. I wanted every reader to know exactly what they needed to do to win an incentive trip when they finished this book. You will.

I've seen so many wonderful trips offered by various companies over the years, but never found a book or training on how to win one. I knew this book could fill a niche, but as I delved deeper into the writing process, I had the same experience as with my previous writing efforts. The book began to take on a life of its own. Things I hadn't planned on including initially began to occur to me and found their way into the pages, making it so much more than the "1-2-3 GO!" narrative I had envisioned in the beginning. I wanted to give you more.

This is a step-by-step plan for earning an incentive trip with your company, with a touchy-feely twist. It is also my story. After 2 years of having fun and doing minimal work with my company, I was ready for more. I had been around the block in the direct sales industry. Now, I wanted the fairy tale. The fairy tale is tough to get. In fairy tales, the heroine has to go through major obstacles, dangers. and heartaches before the dream comes true. Overcoming these makes the dream all the sweeter in the end! Reading this book, however, will help you avoid at least a few of the dragons.

Although my focus is showing you how to earn trip promotions, you can use the following strategies to achieve any of your business goals. If travel is your jam, this book is definitely for you! But what if you crave the recognition your company offers – a certain prestigious title, level, or achievement for which you will receive on-stage recognition at the next big convention or training? Maybe you have a financial goal – to pay off your mortgage, save for a new car, or get out of credit card debt. Perhaps jewelry, a car, or other material incentives are being offered. You can achieve all of these with my system. Whether your company calls you a director, a consultant, a representative, a distributor, or something else, your heart's desire is attainable! If you don't believe it yet, just trust me, and read on.

You will notice that much of the terminology I use is geared towards home and party sales, but you can easily adapt it to your company. The principles are the same. Sales is sales, and a trip is a trip! One of my greatest sales mentors has been my stepdad, who sold both real estate and insurance for a living, and those are hardly home parties.

One of the best things you will discover during your quest for an incentive trip is all the other exciting rewards in store along the way. Desire is the starting point. Where you are now doesn't matter. The bigger the desire, the sooner you will realize your dream!

If you don't even have desire yet – perhaps only curiosity – guess what. That's ok too! Begin where you are.

WHY TRIPS?

Live with no excuses and **travel** with
no regrets. ~ Oscar Wilde.

Most direct sales and network marketing companies offer fun and glamourous trips as their brass ring, the reward for top performers in sales, recruiting, and team production. There is a good reason why. Most people enjoy vacations and travel! To be handed one for free, and treated like a queen (or king!) is even better! "All expenses paid" is the way to go.

Is an incentive trip for you? If you are willing to give 100% of your time and effort into your business during part or most of the qualifying period, and you are excited to do so; if you want to go beyond the limits you have set for yourself in the past; if you are ready to strike out on new ground and throw out habit and thought patterns that are holding you back; if you are enthusiastically on board, then the answer is YES!!! If you aren't yet ready to do these things, that doesn't mean the answer is automatically a no. You just need to examine carefully how bad you want to accomplish this, what you are willing to sacrifice to do so, and if you want a trip badly enough to do that. If you want it badly enough, you can do what's necessary.

If you are with a business that offers incentive trips, but you have never been on one you are missing out on the magical side of the business. Look at your sales and sponsoring numbers. You may be surprised to see that you are not that far away from being able to qualify. Sometimes just that little extra effort is all it takes.

The trips are indeed fabulous. You may not yet realize that one of the reasons why is the wonderful friends you will make along the way, and especially the lifelong friends you will make on the trip itself. On an incentive trip, you will have only the best in the business as companions! Comparing notes and learning secrets from these other top performers will be one of your most valuable take-aways from this experience. And They will learn from you too! You will bond. You will make memories that will last a lifetime.

But in all my time in the industry, I've noticed that the trips elude the vast majority of representatives. They are supposed to. If everybody could get them, the requirements wouldn't be high enough. Winning a trip means something – you put in the extra effort, you made the sacrifices, you are special. You accomplished something that 98% do not. Only the top performers get the trips. This makes sense, but it always bothered me that more didn't attain them. I'm convinced that if more representatives knew precisely what steps to take to earn the trips and had strategies in place for this goal, we would see many more trip winners. My goal with this book is for you – the reader – to get one.

Some trip promotions are available to all who achieve the requirements, others are open to only the "Top 50" or even "First Top 5" who hit the mark. Some are for the representative only, some allow you to bring guests or family along, or bring a guest of your choice for a specified amount at your own expense. Some trips are included when you achieve a certain level or title with the company. Whatever the requirements, they are free, fabulous trips!

Over the years, many of the consultants I have spoken with from various companies don't even consider working for a travel incentive. As soon as they look at the requirements, they dismiss it as out of their reach. (I did too as a new consultant.) Others think that although they might be able to pull it off, they don't want to work that hard, or worse, work hard and then not quite make the cut. They would love to have a trip incentive, but not everything they have to do to get it.

Winning a trip is not easy – you have to hit big numbers. But the reward when you are on that beach or ship or enjoying that luxury accommodation is so huge, you will forget all about the late-night drives home after your party, or the headaches such as cancellations and undependable hostesses, or that school event you may have missed to reach your goal. Once on the trip, you will know in your heart it was worth every difficulty and sacrifice. And you will want more!

Will you have the motivation to go for it – to give it all you've got? Even if you only treat yourself to one incentive trip, you owe it to yourself to have this over-the-top experience at least once. You have nothing to lose.

MY FIRST TRIP

Don't listen to what they say, go see.
~ Chinese Proverb

"Do you even remember your first trip?" I was talking to Melissa, one of my big heroines in the business. I ran into her at our annual conference. I was in awe of her. The trip bug had recently bitten me, and I knew Melissa was one of our huge winners. I only knew her from the training DVDs our company put out for new consultants. She was at the top of the company and had won multiple trips all over the world. It had not gone to her head. She was still down to earth and easy to approach. I'll always remember her answer to me that day. "Yes. And it will always be a very special memory." I wanted to be just like her! Hard-working and successful, with a super-sweet and helpful spirit. I couldn't have chosen a better role model. Others would show up along my journey.

Winning the next incentive trip with my company was my big dream. I was a total sucker for the glamourous, full-color trip promos from the corporate office tempting us to achieve trips. I had been in direct sales with another company years before, and had dreamed of going on the trips then, but could never even get close. This time would be different. I knew I could do it if I stepped up my game. I was determined and knew this was the company where I could do it. After talking with Melissa, my desire was even stronger. How I wanted to be where she was!!! Although I still have not achieved that, I did realize my dream of many trips.

The incentive trip for the first quarter that year was the spa trip to The Phoenician in Scottsdale, Arizona – a 5-star luxury resort whose spa offered not only a buffet menu of different kinds of massages, facial and body treatments, and pedicures, but also meditation classes, hikes, and a variety of fitness options. These fabulous treats were included with our trip, along with gourmet meals, pool time with private cabanas, and even spending money! It was the ultimate in spoiling for those who qualified. Sign me up!

Having never won a trip before, where was I to begin? I was in a "party plan" company specializing in spa, beauty, fragrance, and intimacy products which shone best at the traditional "in-home" party. Earning the incentive trip began and ended with how many parties I was able to crank out in that first 3 months of the year. The sales and sponsoring numbers were steep – much higher than I had ever produced before. My work was cut out for me.

The fact that I was one of our few consultants in my whole

state was an advantage. Many people hadn't even heard of my company where I lived, so it was almost like having a whole new company to promote. The field was wide open.

Hitting the ground running, I had tunnel vision. I don't even remember now how they notified me I had qualified. That first qualification period is a total blur. But I do remember arriving at The Phoenician. I was the first one of the trip winners to get there, and corporate representatives were ready to greet me and show me around. A wonderful lady named Glenda took me out onto the veranda overlooking the beautifully manicured grounds below dotted with the many fancy pools and hot tubs, with the spa in the distance. As we stood there on the veranda of the main building, I teared up. There was a lot to come, but right now just standing on the veranda with Glenda was enough. She noticed my emotion and was quick to tell me, "You earned it."

Every incentive trip since, I have enjoyed that magical moment – in the pool on the cruise ship setting sail for the Bahamas, on the balcony outside my room at Disney's Animal Kingdom Lodge with my little granddaughter, watching the giraffes and zebras roaming below, running into the surf in Cancun with my new friend and roommate, to name a few– I'M HERE! After months of hard consistent effort, you deserve your moment.

Our first night in Arizona an elegant, outdoor welcome cocktail reception with the president of our company and also our founder and CEO was held for us. This is where I met some of the ladies I had been admiring from afar for months with their tremendous accomplishments in their businesses. I was pinching myself.

Phoenix was everything I had envisioned, and so much more. I did it all. Horseback riding through the desert with my private guide, hiking to the top of Camelback Mountain, attending the guided meditation class at the spa, taking a private fitness class, all our planned elegant meals and activities, and of course plenty of pool time with our private cabanas. My roommate was Amber from the east coast. We did a lot together, even finding time to check out a Scottsdale thrift store. We squeezed in as much as we could.

Getting ready to leave on the final morning was a bittersweet moment. I was sorry the trip was ending, but also ready to get home and jump right into working for the next trip. I was hooked.

THE BEST COMPANY FOR YOU

Time flies. It's up to you to be the navigator. ~ Robert Orben

I was fortunate enough to be with a fantastic company when I set my sights on that first trip but had paid my dues with several others first. Having the right company was a major factor in my success. With my first company, the trips had been completely out of my reach. No matter how hard I worked, even becoming a car-winning leader, the trip incentives eluded me – and I CRAVED them. I had thought that since the products and marketing plan were great I could accomplish anything, not knowing that the deck was stacked against me from the start. I learned the hard way that having a great company and working hard wasn't enough.

Perhaps you are already in a company that you love and are ready to go for their incentive trip for the first time. I'm here to help you do that. Maybe you don't even have a company yet. What if you have several you are considering for your direct sales business? How do you make sure you are choosing one where achieving the trips is attainable for you? I'm not going to tell you to choose one company over another. I won't make it that easy. I have my preferences when it comes to products, marketing plans, and business methods. But you need to make the best decision for you, not me. You want to find a place where you can shine your brightest and use all your natural gifts. At the same time, I'd like to spare you the frustration I experienced with that first go-round which had left me discouraged and disenchanted about the direct sales industry.

First, figure out what you like. What are you passionate about? What company appeals to you right away? To get the big numbers required for a trip, you are going to have to enjoy what you are doing and believe in it. Pick something you like! Research several companies online, or talk to people you know who are representatives in companies you are thinking about. If you know you like their products, find out about their marketing plan, and specifically about their trip offerings. What current incentive trips are they promoting? Find out what the requirements are to attain them. What is the profit potential (that is, what is your discount percentage on products)? Are you able to get products for yourself at a discount in addition to your sales orders, and have those count towards your trip too? Are you able to build a team? All of these details make a difference. Look at the fine print before you sign. Compare.

Companies usually announce their travel promotions

a month or so ahead of the date when you can begin qualifying for them. The incentives you are looking at might be starting soon, several months from now, or even next year. That's ok – although some consultants join and win a trip almost immediately, having some time to train and get your feet wet is beneficial too. You can be that much further ahead when the qualification period arrives. Perhaps a promotion just ended. One of the nice things about incentive trips is, there is always another one coming up. It may be next quarter or next year, but there is always a travel incentive on the horizon. Your time will come.

One of the factors in choosing the best company as the vehicle for you to win a trip is, how many others are with them, especially in your area? It may be discouraging for you to find out that another consultant for that brand shows up every time you turn around. No matter how much you like that jewelry, or skincare, or weight loss supplement if they are well-established and your town is pretty well sewn up, it may be harder for you to get started. Every time you reach out, you may find your prospect already has a representative.

My first home-sales company had so many consultants in a small town, I had set myself up for a hard time without realizing it. I still achieved a lot but could have done much better in a company with fewer representatives in town, as I proved years later. Many people hadn't even heard my next company yet. The opportunity was wide open for both sales and recruiting. Also, my products were not readily available just down the street. I appreciated all the great training and friendships from that first company, but when I found my current one, it was like night and day as far as what I could achieve. The number of consultants does make a difference.

You may still want to choose a popular company – that is fine, as long as you know going in that you may run into a lot of competition. You can win a trip with ANY company – but you may excel in some better and quicker than others. Just go in with your eyes wide open.

Most companies require you to buy a "starter" kit which contains the supplies and products you need to promote your new business, whether through home parties or online, the 2 main ways direct sales businesses are done. How much do you have to invest in such a kit? Some companies cost less than $50 to start, some several thousand or more. The start-up cost shouldn't be your main consideration, but it is certainly an important one. You may even have several price options to choose from for your kit purchase. Be clear on what you get and what you are spending before you commit.

You will probably have a "sponsor" or "upline" – the person with whom you signed your agreement. Training, meetings, and events are offered with most companies to support your business – giving recognition, ideas, friendship, and fun! Winning a trip isn't all work. You will have lots of fun on the way to your goal! If you don't, you are doing something wrong. You should be having the time of your life! All sponsors have different styles and personalities. Try to pick someone you know you will enjoy working with, perhaps even one who has won trips herself. A great sponsor can be a huge factor in your success.

Having said that, some representatives who have no sponsor still make it to the top and win the big trips. Their sponsor may have quit or they may have signed directly under the corporate office. The main ingredient for winning your trip is your desire, no matter what your sponsor situation. Just make sure you connect with someone who will encourage and support you along the way, whether she is your sponsor or not. You may already have this person, but if not you can find her. Keep your eyes open.

Will the products sell? My preference is a company with offerings to fit all budgets. If you have only one product to sell and the price point is several thousand dollars, you may be going a long time between sales. If the same or similar product is available for less at the local discount store this is something to consider too. Anything that will hurt your sales potential is a factor to weigh in your decision. If 10 other home sales companies have similar items, YOU may think your's is the best, but you will have lots of competition. Does the company require customers to "sign up" for some kind of auto-ship or club to get a better price? Some people like this and some don't. DO YOUR HOMEWORK before signing.

Keeping all these points in mind, if one company particularly stands out to you, you get a good vibe, and you have done your homework, it is time to take the plunge! You only have so much time before that trip qualification period begins – maybe it already has!

Once you have selected your company, you can begin working for your trip goal, even if the contest period hasn't started yet! The trips are within reach for absolutely anyone who is willing to put in the effort and who is with a company that makes them achievable. I'm going to show you how.

GETTING READY

The gladdest moment in human
life is a departure into unknown
lands. ~ Sir Richard Burton

Let's take a sample trip promotion and break the requirements down into smaller parts. This trip will be Hawaii for 2 – but we are just playing, so make it anywhere you want! You need $90,000 in retail sales during the qualification period as well as 24 new consultants/ representatives added to your team. We will use one year as our sample qualification period. You can adjust this easy formula for a 3, 4, or 6-month period as well. For our sample trip, we'll say that an unlimited number of distributors can qualify. Each company will be a little different, but this will give you the basic idea.

$90,000 broken down into 12 monthly parts is $7500 per month in retail sales. If you are a realtor or insurance sales representative, your requirements will look different. Perhaps it will be so many homes sold or so many new policies written. Whatever it is, break it down by the month first. Sales often fluctuate by the time of year. For example, in the romance business, I know I can count on a high month right before Valentine's. Even should another emergency happen, and we have to go to all online appointments, as happened in 2020, this will still be the case. Many consultants in my company routinely do $10-$20,000 per month in sales, but for many $7500 is a stretch. For our sample trip, we'll say that we may have a couple of lower months in the $3500 range, and some higher ones in the $10,000 range. We can allow for those, and just make sure they average out to $7500 per month.

The next step is figuring out how many appointments per month you need to reach your sales goal. Figure this based on your per appointment sales average (which hopefully will be going up!). Schedule at least 2 more appointments/parties than you think you need to reach your monthly total allowing for cancellations and no-shows. For many businesses working at the trip-winning level is at least 10-12 parties per month, plus reorders, website purchases, and of course, sponsoring. If this is about right for you, book 15-18 appointments per month. Some representatives have a much higher average per appointment and prefer to do fewer parties per month, but when working for a trip I don't like to count on the sales of any one party. A fuller calendar gives me a higher comfort level. Besides, some months you might not get your 15-18 appointments. Shoot for that amount anyway.

Sponsoring is easier to figure out. 2 per month equals your 24! But don't shoot for 24. Shoot for at least double that amount. This will help you build your team more quickly anyway. Never shoot for your minimum trip numbers, in sponsoring or sales. Always aim for higher. We'll talk more about the specifics of sponsoring later.

Now refigure the numbers you came up with for 10-11-months rather than for a full year. This allows for the unexpected and gives you a little wiggle room. You could have a year that runs smoothly, but don't count on it. Plan for a shorter length of time to give yourself a little flexibility. If you complete the qualifications within that shorter time, you still have a month or 2 to work! If not, you have that extra month you need.

Just like I did with the Disney World trip (see My Ultimate – Disney World) front-load yourself with appointments early on. The Magic 5 chapter will show you how to make sure you have your calendar full when you begin. Getting even more specific, most requirements begin the first month of the year. This means you want your January full of clients before Christmas – then do a special promotion the last part of December to fill in any gaps. For this promotion, give something extra special. Give away the farm if you have to. Make sure your January is packed. It will pay off later. From these appointments, you can make others for February and March. Ideally, you have already done several events (see the Magic 5!) and connected with the chambers and leads group before December.

Once your calendar is full, begin your hostess coaching to make sure these parties or shows take place! This part is so crucial, a whole chapter is devoted to it later as well as a wonderful book on hostess coaching in the resources section!

If you begin to feel overwhelmed at any point, and if you are doing this right you might consider hiring an assistant. You don't have to pay big bucks. Perhaps someone on your team or a friend will help you with mailings and posting on your party events in exchange for products or a combination of products and an hourly fee. Get creative, but make it worth their while. This will free you up to get twice the work done.

Remember that your new team member prospects will come from these first appointments too. Be prepared by ordering plenty of sponsoring literature in advance. If your prospect signs early in the year, she may be eligible for the trip incentive too! Dangle it in front of her! Seeing your new consultant achieve something like this will give you so much pride and satisfaction, and get her business off to an amazing start!

The key is to begin implementing all the ideas in this book before that qualification period begins. Having said that, I have been on trips where I met consultants who signed up in January and won the same trip I did! Not everyone has to plan, but that is how I am wired, and everyone can benefit from doing so. The more you do ahead of time, the more you can focus on the tasks at hand.

Feel free to make a diagram to chart your progress. Now that you have the numbers worked out, we're going to look at some other preparation tips and start you on your way! Better go buy a guide book for your trip!

STARTING STRATEGIES

I was alone, I took a ride, I didn't know what I would find there. ~ The Beatles

One of the cool things about setting your sights on an incentive trip is, the goal is set for you! Your company tells you right upfront what you have to do and when! All you need to do is break the numbers down into bite-sized pieces and do the work. This truly is as simple as it sounds. Take a look at what you already did in the last quarter or 2. Then do the math: how much more do you have to accomplish in sales and sponsoring numbers to get to that trip goal, and what is the time limit? You may be surprised to see that with just an extra appointment or 2 a month, the trip may be attainable for you. If you are brand new and don't yet have a track record, you can still break down the requirements and be ready to go.

Even if you look at the numbers and realize you need to double, or even triple, what you have done before don't let that scare you. It will be a challenge, but you know what you have to do and that is the first step. Now, how do you achieve these big numbers?

1. <u>Tell people what you are doing!</u> Shout it from the rooftops! Get excited! That excitement will take you a long way. Plus, once you tell everyone, you feel you have to follow through. As you make your calls or send your texts and instant messages, don't be afraid to say why you need an appointment! Whether it is a one-on-one to share samples of your health and weight-loss supplements, an appointment to host an in-home party, or an invitation to a sponsoring evening, you can use the same basic script. "Sue I'm so excited! I'm working for a Mediterranean Cruise! I need to start the quarter with some awesome parties, and I thought of you right away. We've been meaning to set a date, and the timing is perfect because we are having a new product launch too. I've got a killer hostess special for the ladies who help me towards my goal." Those in insurance or some other non-party business will word it differently, but you get the idea.

   Your trip goal gives you a new reason to call those you haven't talked to in a while. Think of past party hostesses as well as new prospects when you plan your contacts. Try saying, "I know you must be out of shaving cream by now. Let's get it for you free!" "It's time to do our year-end review on your policy!"

When getting close to completing your requirements, you can say, "I am so close! I just need 2 more parties (or appointments) to reach the cruise!!!" One special memory when I was working for the Bahamas Cruise, was just a small party. Only 2 ladies attended, and one didn't stay very long. I had driven 6 hours to this party and had hoped for more attendance, but I resolved to have fun and not worry about the results. Then something wonderful happened. The hostess not only surprised me by signing up with our largest starter kit, she then proceeded to place her first consultant order. As if that wasn't enough, she asked, "What else can I do to help you get The Bahamas???" People LOVE to help you get your trip! This is not something you do alone. It is a team effort: hostesses, clients, new consultants, and possibly your team as well. Don't try to go it alone. Get them all involved and excited with you!

Remember the importance of sponsoring! Many trips require you to add to your team. Is there someone who has been thinking about the opportunity you have to offer? Now is the time to follow up with them. Going for a trip gives you the perfect reason to contact them again. Tell them what you are doing! If your prospect isn't quite ready to sign with you, offer them a fantastic hostess deal. Ask them for a referral of anyone who might like to either party or sign with you. More on sponsoring later, but get your mind working in that direction now.

2. Motivate Your Team - Some trip incentives have a team production requirement. How do you motivate them to achieve right along with you? Make it worth their while. If there was ever a time for a team incentive, this is it! Offer something special and be generous. Your special promotion should be a challenge but achievable, just like winning the trip!

   Let everybody win. Whoever qualifies gets the prize, no limit. This way, your team member is only competing against herself.

   Perhaps your team members are eligible to earn the same trip for which you are working or a similar one. Inspire them to go for it! Read this book together and have a strategy meeting to make your plans. Your team grows and succeeds along with you, and if you are a good leader, you will find it means almost as much to you to help them win as it does to win yourself. That is the way direct sales is designed to work.

   If you know she is working for a promotion, send her something to inspire and encourage her. Make a collage, or send a notebook with "Dreams Come True" on the cover and a personal note from you. These little gestures mean a lot, and they are rare. You want to make your team member feel special just like your hostesses. Check in with her when she reaches a milestone or hits an obstacle. Be her biggest cheerleader.

3. <u>Get your family on board.</u> I have yet to see someone succeed whose husband wasn't supportive – or at least tolerant – of what his wife was doing. This most likely works the other way too if you are a guy reading this book. Working for a goal like this is challenging enough without having opposition at home. Get them on your side.

   If you have a supportive partner, fantastic! Having them in your corner is a tremendous advantage! There are times during the process when you may need to say, I love you and I'll see you in a week! If your week, or even your month, are packed with appointments, let them know ahead of time. Let everyone know how they can pitch in during your super-push times – and promise them something special at the end!

   Most successful representatives have supportive families behind them (or no family, so no one to worry about). I always tell loved ones what I am working for. I tell them not to spring anything on me that I need to attend – give me notice, or I just may not be able to make it. Then, I remind them. They know when I am working for a trip! Communication is the key – bribery works too! You know your family, and you can find a way. Do this ahead of time, and you will be glad you did.

If you need more than this to convince your family or partner what is important to you, you may need a different book. If it is that hard, this may be your biggest hurdle – and one you may need help overcoming. Achieving a huge goal without the support of those close to you is possible – but you have a strike against you, and you don't need that going into this.

THE MAGIC FIVE

It is a common mistake to overestimate one's potential free time and consequently overpack. In travel, as in most of life, less is invariably more. ~William Hurt, "The Accidental Tourist"

> If you are cheating and skipping to one section, this should be it. These are the steps that will get you to bigger numbers than you have ever had before. The key is, you have to work them every day to make things happen. So let's go!

One sentence I have heard many times as a leader is "But I don't know anyone!" Aside from this being untrue, let's look at what she may mean.

1. I just moved to a new area and haven't met anyone yet. (A perfect opportunity, by the way.)
2. My family and friends have all said no or are uninterested. (I've been there.)
3. I don't have any friends. (If this is true, you need to make some!)

4. I'm new to the business and don't yet have a clientele to ask or call. (We all had to start somewhere.)
5. Someone else already has all the business in this town. (Usually a big excuse.)
6. I don't have a team yet. (Prospects are everywhere!)

Whether or not any or all of the above statements apply to you and your business, you need to find some new people! You ALWAYS need to be finding new people, but during trip-winning time it is especially important. After stating the obvious, let's take a look at the best and quickest ways to infuse your business with new blood.

Jill's Magic Five:

1. People in daily life
2. Events
3. Chambers of Commerce
4. Online marketing methods
5. Networking/Leads groups

Tens of thousands of people in sales and other kinds of businesses use these every day and have used them for decades. I'm just the one putting them together in regards specifically to earning incentive trips. I'll go out on a limb and say that if you do these five, consistently and enthusiastically, you will reach your goal. You will be stronger in some of the Magic Five than in others – you may particularly excel at one or two. But don't neglect the others. Improving in them may be just the thing your business needs.

As you use these five avenues, you will find that other opportunities to meet new people will come your way, seemingly like magic! Well, it IS the Magic Five! And it will start you on your way to big numbers.

Use the Magic Five ideas, whether or not you have exhausted the "warm market" of people around you – friends & family mainly. In building my team, this scenario repeated itself so many times: My new team member would come to the end of people she knew, and wasn't successful in finding new ones – but not if she was practicing the Magic Five! You will be ahead of the game when you run out of people you know.

The good news is the Magic Five work for anyone, anywhere. Even in Antarctica, you could use some of these options! If you get creative, you can adapt them to "distancing" guidelines and similar restrictions as well. We'll begin with the cheapest method which absolutely anyone can do.

1. People in Daily Life – Marketing your business as you go about your daily life makes sense. People are everywhere and you may have just the thing they've been looking for, either as an opportunity or with your products. Of the five in the Magic Five, this is the cheapest and least time-consuming way of finding new clients. The results can be amazing if you do it consistently. The keyword is consistently.

    You won't get an appointment or sale every time you talk to someone, so doing it daily, routinely, and habitually, is key. So where are these people? Everywhere!

Although you may want to target prospects based on your company's products or opportunity, don't neglect others. In my current company we mainly work with women eighteen and older – but remember, they have husbands and boyfriends. Make sure that handyman doesn't leave your home without your business card, and possibly a catalog if he wants it, and a sample for his wife or girlfriend. Your approach doesn't have to be awkward or intrusive. Sometimes you may just say, "May I give you one of my cards?" No one has ever said no to me.

Get into the simple habit of wearing your name badge. This alone will get people's attention. I always read people's badges, don't you? I have gotten parties and even new team members just from wearing my badge. Don't depend on it though. Find creative and natural ways to bring your business up in conversations.

Go to new places! While I was building up my sales business, still working my day job, I would challenge myself to hand out a certain number of cards every lunch hour in town. I had to think of new places to go, and new people to meet as I quickly ran out of my usual places. Servers and cashiers are popular but think of vet's offices, salons (tanning, nail, hair, massage), real estate offices where you can go to ask questions. Go in for legitimate reasons, not just to solicit. This kind of interaction will be limited during times of Covid restriction, but that won't last forever. In the meantime, do your best.

Have inexpensive things to have done in the salon, such as a toe polish change. If you are a guy, get a mani/pedi! You have to get out there too. This isn't just for the women! Guys win trips too! But none of this works unless you strike up a conversation. Start by saying I want my toes to look good for my party I'm doing tonight. Or, what do you have for a more dramatic look? I have this event I'm doing...Most people will then ask you about your upcoming appointment. This gets easier as you get into the habit. Successful salespeople practice talking to people in daily life.

Go into the vet office to buy pet food, or a gift for someone if you don't have a pet yourself. Bring goody bags for the staff. You can also do this at a novelty or bookstore – you name it. Buy a pie at the local diner for your event that night – but make sure you are wearing your name badge and have a goody bag for the server.

Come up with ideas. Make it fun, not a chore. Give yourself a numbers challenge as you go out on errands. Nowhere is off-limits. I don't wear my name badge to church, of course, but I do carry my purse with my company logo on it and people have commented on it. Be sensitive and cordial. Always show respect and courtesy for anyone else's business. Keep in mind, many representatives don't market in daily life. Most consultants don't win trips either. We want you to break out from the pack.

Events

Events are an absolute goldmine. You can succeed without them – but you will succeed quicker and bigger with them! In one event, you can come away with more new names than you would in months of marketing in daily life. What is the downside? Events can be pricey, and some are better than others. You have to check them out in advance, see what events suit your business the best, learn how to work them to your best advantage, and then spend the time and energy necessary to make them a success. They are a lot of work – and worth every bit. If you share them with others, they can be challenging to coordinate. But you can minimize the unpleasant aspects if you set expectations beforehand.

How do you select an event? There are many kinds to choose from. Here are some of the most popular:

Bridal shows & expos

Octoberfests

Community fairs

Park festivals

Holiday craft shows

Church bazaars

Women's Expos

Health Fairs

Farmers Markets

Find out ahead of time what your company's policy is on doing events. Do you have to register the event with your company? Get permission? This is usually pretty simple, but don't skip this step. Is the event exclusive? That is, will you be the only one from your company allowed to be at the event? This is the policy at most events, but make sure. Don't leave things to chance with events. Go over the contract carefully. With many, you will forfeit your payment should the event be canceled due to weather or another act of God. Make sure you are well aware of the policies both of your company and the event promoter before you proceed.

What event will suit you and your budget best? What events are available in your area? Online is the best place to start looking, but also ask around. You may find one or more through a Chamber of Commerce, which we'll cover in the next section. Pick one that looks good, and begin the process. Most will require a deposit in advance. Many events fill up fast and are hard to get into as a vendor due to their popularity.

Bridal shows fit for almost all vendors and companies. They are my favorites, and I do a lot of them. I see everyone there from insurance agents and weight loss companies to romance and kitchen theme companies, wine merchants, make up, and almost everything else. Most promoters provide a list of attendees with their contact information after the show. Some put you on their website or event announcement or give you radio time to promote your business. You may have an opportunity to put your info into the event gift bags that attendees receive. You get a lot with bridal events. They are usually also your most expensive events. They can run from several hundred to several thousand dollars, depending on the show. They also tend to fill up quickly.

The other event categories are usually less expensive than your bridal shows. Some may even be free or very low cost. If you can snag a free or inexpensive show, do so. You have nothing to lose. Shows such as Octoberfests usually won't have attendee information included since they don't have people sign up, but you should always have a way to get contact information at your booth, such as registering attendees for a drawing or giveaway.

Check your event out thoroughly, especially if it is on the pricier side. Has the event been done before? What is their track record for attendance? Does the promoter or organization have a good reputation? How are they advertising the show? What is the venue like? What perks do they offer to go with your booth fee? If it is a new or first-time event, check it out even more. Make sure that the attendance and exposure are worth your investment. Don't learn the hard way like I did.

One of my favorite promoters is planning a "Virtual Drive-Thru" bridal show during our time of social distancing. Since this is a first-time thing, and no one knows how it will turn out, the fee is greatly reduced. If it is not successful, the promoter will apply the entire fee to their next in-person show. This is the kind of promoter you want to work with. I'm doing the event because I can't lose either way and who knows? It could be a great success! Look around for any event deals like this that you can find.

If an event you want is over your budget, explore ways to offset the cost. If it is worth the price, see if the promoter has less expensive options, such as a booth in a less pricey location or a way to "work off" some of the cost by providing ushers or stuffing attendee bags. If you want all the bells and whistles of the more expensive booth, see if other representatives can share with you equally in the cost for an equal sharing of leads obtained from the show.

Once you have done your homework and selected your event, what's next? Learn how to work the event to make it successful. You want to squeeze every drop of benefit from your investment. Does your company have an event guru? Famous for getting great results? Does the promoter offer tips for getting the most value out of the event? Perhaps your company has event tips with which they can provide you. Take advantage of all of this. Go on YouTube and type in bridal shows (or whatever kind of event you are working) and your company's name. See what gems come up. Check with other consultants and see what has worked for them. The more you prepare, the better off you will be when the big day arrives.

Get your supplies together in plenty of time. Avoid the stress of a last-minute rush or trip to the store. If several are working the show, decide who brings what. Don't forget your sign-up slips for the drawing, and your items for the swag bags if you are participating in that!

If your show is large-scale and offers set-up the day before, take advantage of it. You won't always have this luxury. Many expos and events only offer day-of set up during certain hours. Others may be too far away to make swinging by the day before practical. When I have been able to set up in advance, I've been so glad I did. I could set up without rushing and take my time. Then the day of the event, I can walk right in and my booth is ready. Heaven! It seemed like the set-up fairy had come in and done it for me! With a long day ahead, this is a definite plus. I have even been known to go for a set up the day before and spend the night in the venue city just to take advantage of that day-before option.

During the event, be fun, professional, enthusiastic, and outgoing. Don't be caught sitting behind your table looking at your phone or eating! Don't be behind your table at all! The best vendors get out in front of their table and make eye contact with the attendees rather than waiting for them to approach. Don't be aggressive, be assertive. Be charming! This is the time to get out of your comfort zone. You will get a lot of no's today, that goes with the territory. You have to get the no's to get the yesses! Connect with other vendors. Go around with your cards and introduce yourself. This puts you ahead of the game again. Ninety-eight percent of vendors won't bother to do this. Some of my best contacts have been other vendors.

Whatever methods you use to work your event, make sure they result in as many leads as possible. You should always have some kind of door prize or giveaway. Then, FOLLOW UP!!! And do so within twenty four hours – that night or the next day if at all possible. Don't let the excitement fade. I do my drawing the night of the event if I can, otherwise the next morning, and text or call my drawing winners right away. There are many options for prizes – but always make sure to award any prizes offered. DON'T YOU DARE offer prizes and not give them out! This is false advertising, and could even get you into trouble with the event organizer. I normally give away more than one prize. I like to do 2 grand prizes, 2-3 first prizes, and then the rest receive my second prize. They receive their prize at their follow-up appointment or party. We tell them this when they register for the drawing so there is no misunderstanding.

Some vendors pull the bait & switch, saying that you have won a prize, but then putting a condition on it during the follow-up call. If there is a condition to receiving the prize, tell people upfront. Don't save this information for later. That is a turn-off. If I have "won" a certain supply of food, or makeup, or whatever, great! Then I get it! But if you say that is the prize "with a 6-month membership" tell me when I register for the drawing. At my booth, we say that you need to select a party date when you register for the drawing, which can be changed later if needed, and you get the prize at your party. Then they know the terms. Have this all set in advance with everyone working the event.

Be excited and friendly on your follow-up calls, but have a script from which to work too to keep you on track. You will have a lot of calls to make, and you want great results, so find out the wording that has worked well for others in your business. Don't sound like you are reading. Practice until you feel natural saying the words.

Shoot for working an event or two before your trip qualification period begins, and use them to help fill your calendar. Work events during the qualification period too. The longest qualification period I have seen is one year, and during that time you will want to do several events. Perhaps some big, some smaller, some that you may have even put on yourself! If you only have three months in which to win, however, time is of the essence. Work your events in advance and begin that time period with your book full.

Remember your goal – more leads, more names, more business, more sales, more sponsoring. These are the things that will get you to your cruise ship, island, or luxury resort!

Chambers of Commerce

Another incredible resource of new leads, events, and support for your business, Chambers of Commerce are the most overlooked by direct sellers of the Magic 5. They often think of Chambers as something that is only for "real businesses", or as an unnecessary expense that won't benefit their business. If you have been guilty of this thinking, think again. Chambers exist to support businesses and the local community and are almost everywhere you go. Their benefits often include free or low-cost meeting/conference rooms and kitchen facilities, networking events, leads groups, in-person and online training, the opportunity to display your business information or cards, and much more. They are worth checking out. If you decide a certain chamber is not a good fit for you, you can move on to another. You are not limited to one chamber either, once you find one you like. There may be several that interest you within a half-hour drive.

But look before you leap. Chambers are easy to look into without investing any money, or at least not much. Your first step is to call for an appointment with the membership person. Allow about half an hour for your meeting with them and bring a professional-looking portfolio with your business information: catalog, business card, leaflets, and brochures. Wear your name badge, and don't go in jeans, even if those in the chamber are wearing them. Make a professional first impression.

The neat thing about this meeting is, you are expected to talk about your business! You don't need to think of a clever way to bring it up in conversation. You are there to talk about it! Be honest and direct about what you are looking for from the chamber. If this is your first chamber, be inquisitive, and see what they have to offer you. Saying you are new to the area (if that is true) or new to chambers and want to boost your business is a good way to begin. Even if you get a good vibe, don't sign up right then. You want a reason for a second meeting – a second chance to stop by. Make sure you inquire about any upcoming events the chamber may be sponsoring to see if they interest you and whether membership is required to participate.

Your next step is to attend one of the chamber's get-acquainted or networking functions. Most have a monthly breakfast get together with a short program put on by one of the member businesses. You will have an opportunity to give your short "commercial" – so have it ready and look your best. Evening receptions are usually offered at least once a month at little or no charge. This is your chance to mingle, network, and get a feel for the other member businesses. Attend one or 2 of these before going back to the office to join. Have your radar up for businesses you may want to use yourself, rather than just thinking about your own. Don't be one of those who are just out for themselves and not interested in supporting others. The magic comes in when we all support each other.

Should you decide this chamber is not for you, at least you had a chance to make some connections, meet some "people in daily life", hand out some cards and goody bags, and possibly even make some appointments. You may decide to try a couple more functions before joining or move on to another chamber.

Depending on your business, you may even sell something on the spot when going into the office or attending one of the functions. Be ready! Be open to what the chamber has to offer. Don't feel obligated to join, but consider the possibility.

Whether you end up being a chamber member or not, you have to admit you have met more people, all in the context of marketing your business. Occasionally you may run across a chamber that doesn't accept home sales businesses – most do, but the others may still have a spot for you to display your literature or cards. And another chamber is always out there!

My team members know not to tell me they "can't get any parties" or "don't know anyone" if they haven't checked out a local chamber or two.

Internet Marketing

Before you think that this section goes without saying, keep in mind that believe it or not people are still out there who are babes in the woods when it comes to using the internet, let alone using it to market a business. Some refuse to have a Facebook or Instagram page. I understand but get on the internet anyway. It is a necessity for marketing your business.

You can reach more prospects faster with internet marketing than you can even with events, and can often do so free of charge! You may already be an online marketing whiz – if so, you are ahead of the game. You may have much to learn. No matter your starting point, you can accomplish a lot with the internet!

Social media has been important in business marketing for years but became crucial during COVID 19 times. Those of us in the home party and other businesses requiring public contact had to temporarily shift over to online and "virtual". It was good for us. We learned how much we could accomplish online. For those already doing this a lot, a big shift wasn't necessary. The rest of us were thrown into the deep end of the pool. Most of us learned to swim very quickly. Adapt or die!

COVID lockdowns are easing in some areas for the time being, but the future is still uncertain. Internet skills and marketing methods are crucial no matter what happens. Many grew up with them. But if you grew up with a TV that had to warm up for 5 minutes, and had a little dot in the middle as I did...if your first TV memory other than Captain Kangaroo is Kennedy's Cuban Missile Crisis speech...if you remember where you were during his assassination, then you have had more of a learning curve.

Fortunately, many internet skills can be learned for free and are not difficult. I learned most of mine by doing, and asking for help. Books are out there to help you, so are friends and others in your company. Many companies have internet marketing classes through webinars and at their national trainings and conventions. Take advantage of as much as you can for free. This only makes sense before you decide if you need a program or course for which you will get charged.

What about programs you see promoted on Facebook, Youtube, and pop-ups in-between plays on Words With Friends? Do they work? Do they deliver what they promise? What about "Attraction Marketing" techniques and similar programs which advertise amazing numbers of leads coming your way and that you will never have to approach strangers in daily life again? These often try to get your attention with photos of silly looks from the promoter and their kids or slick montages.

All of these programs offer free webinars or tutorials for which they want you to reserve a spot. If one appeals to you, reserve your spot and show up. Continue to watch and learn from anything you can do for free. But beware – at the end of the webinar is the pitch, usually with a ticking clock that gives you a limited time to sign up for and pay for their program. Don't feel pressured and don't sign up immediately. Here is the secret: most of them won't let you go easily. They will be back with another offer just as good or even better after the clock runs out, perhaps the next day. Take your time. Before making your decision remember my mantra – do your homework. Check the program out with your company and other representatives you know. Try to find someone who has used the program. Most of these programs are a real investment. Like events, they run from several hundred to several thousand dollars, so don't jump too quickly.

One program that looked good to me had so many complaints with the Better Business Bureau that I felt uneasy. Any company or program can get a complaint, but when there are a lot of them, that is a red flag.

Having said that, some great programs are out there that may suit you and your business. Many of the techniques they teach can also be learned for free if you apply yourself. Whether you decide to use a fancy program or not, you must market online regularly and strongly, and in an appealing way. Your company could be your best resource for social media marketing. If you need more, endless other learning options exist.

Social Media is a perfect place to let people know about your trip goal and do special promotions for your customers to help you achieve it. The possibilities are truly endless. I'm leaving this a little open-ended for a reason. You will learn a lot from exploring the world of social media marketing on your own. Once you do, remember things out in cyberspace are changing all the time. Trying to keep up can make your head spin. But you don't have to always be doing the latest thing to succeed either.

Find what works for you and stick with it, but also try new ideas. You never know what post will bring leads for you. Keep up with your company's social media techniques and posts. But beware of spending too much time on social media. You can easily cross the line from productive time into wasting huge amounts of time, and during trip qualifications, you don't have time to waste.

Networking and Leads Groups

Like Chambers, networking and leads groups expect you to promote your business right out of the gate. Many offer the opportunity to attend their functions for free the first time or two to try them out. Of course, they are hoping you'll join. But whether you join or not, you will get the word out about your business to a whole new market.

Don't overthink which group might be the best for you. Try several! Then try more! Most chambers have them, others you can easily find online or by asking around. Some are formal groups you have to join for a fee, others offer regular events that you can attend for a small charge each time – usually including breakfast, lunch, or cocktails & snacks. Some have strict requirements for their members about attendance and providing leads to other members, others have none.

Be careful about any group offering "free" networking. Some of these are fronts designed just for members from another company to try and sign you up. Go in with your eyes open. If someone proposes a one-on-one meeting with you following a get-together, make sure it is a true one-on-one where you each get to share your business, not just an opportunity to be exposed to their sign-up pitch.

Check with members (and past members) of groups that interest you. Find out all you can. One group that I liked initially offered the opportunity to substitute for a regular member when needed rather than joining. This sounded great until one of the members told me bluntly that she would never do business with me unless I joined. That was the last time I went as a "substitute". I also spoke with past members and the feedback was that after the initial month or two, the leads weren't quality. People were giving them just to fill a square. I passed on this expensive group.

Another referral group I tried and liked a lot had just one problem. No one was giving any referrals out! After six months, I mentioned it and said that as much as I liked the people in the group, I had joined for party referrals and was getting none, even though I was doing business with most of the other members myself. Nothing changed and I decided not to renew. I'm glad I went and I still do business with some of the other members. It was worthwhile, but I got no referrals. One member even told me it was a "conflict of interest" for her to do business with me or refer anyone to me, even though we were in completely different businesses. Make sure you will get something out of the group into which you put your time and money.

So if I had those experiences, why am I recommending leads groups in the Magic Five? Because other groups are out there! Because you will benefit from your investigation and trying out different groups. Because this is a place to practice your marketing skills. Because you may meet just the person who is looking for you. Because you may meet just the person who has what you need. Just do your homework before joining.

Lastly, if you can find a 5-minute networking, or something similar, go!!!! This is like speed dating for business and you will get fantastic practice giving your commercial. These events are affordable. You will meet perhaps thirty different people in an hour, and can even do this on an extended lunch break if it is close enough to your day job. You are not asked to join anything, and you will have fun!

Start networking!

NEW YORK CITY

The smart traveler must be prepared to make last-minute adjustments. - Dexter Morgan, "Dexter" Season 7, Episode 1

When traveling, expect the unexpected! This was especially true of our New York City shopping spree trip. Although I had spent a lot of time in the city as a flight attendant, even having a place near the United Nations complex, I was always ready to go back. Glamourous, historical, and complex, New York City is like no other city in the world. Everywhere you look, you see famous sights and recognize movie locations from your favorite films. The excitement and energy are contagious.

We weren't just going to go sightseeing, though. We were being given a shopping spree! Or so we thought. Even my wonderful company couldn't control the weather.

As we enjoyed our elegant dinner at the Mandarin the first night of our trip, we already knew that our trip was probably going to be cut short. Hurricane Irene was coming our way. The city that never sleeps for all intents and purposes would close down. They decided to fly us out of the city on the private jets leased by our company the next morning. I considered this to be as exciting as the shopping spree! Not many consultants won the trips, and even fewer got to ride on the private jets. This was the only option if we wanted to get out of town. The jets were lined up on the runway as we scrambled to beat the weather. We made it out just ahead of Jimmy Buffet and his entourage. Everybody who could do so was leaving.

Not quite knowing where to take us, they flew us to Cincinnati, home of our corporate headquarters. There, we could shop, go to a casino, or as my roommate and I did, take a carriage ride around the city. We were still given a super-sumptuous meal that night at one of Cincinnati's best. And we still had our shopping spree money. Not the trip we had planned, but still one with great memories.

As if that wasn't enough in the category of unexpected events, the next morning our airport van was late, making some of us miss our flights. I spent most of the day at the Dayton airport while they tried to figure out what to do with me. Finally that evening, a plane needed to be positioned in Denver, and that became the ticket out for me and a couple of other travelers stuck in Dayton, Ohio. They put us in first class on the empty jet, and we flew back in style.

Knowing New York City as I did from my airline days, at least I had been able to take my excited roommate Valerie, who had never been, around on that one afternoon we had and show her Grand Central Station, and the lions at the New York City public library, made famous at the beginning of Ghostbusters. I pointed out various movie locations as she shot photos. Although our time was short, we still became great friends. Another perfect roommate choice. In all my years of winning trips, the "roommate streak" of fantastic ladies has not been broken. I still don't know how our CEO does it, but he has blessed me with the best roommates every time. I couldn't have chosen better myself!

Even though we had been derailed by the weather, we still had an unforgettable time. The hard work had paid off once again.

THE NUTCRACKER – THE POWER OF THE VISUAL

Travel winning tip: "Make the mental decision to do it. Trips very rarely happen by accident and you have to decide you're going to go and then plan and everyday envision yourself already there with the person/people who you want to be there with and make it happen." Lissa Leona, Touchstone Crystal Jewelry by Swarovski

"So, how did you do it???" I was talking to one of the other "dance moms" from my daughter's studio. They had done a contest to see who could sell the most tickets to our annual Nutcracker. Emily had a major part, the Chinese solo. The contest prize would be free private lessons! I wanted to win the contest! "You won't believe me if I tell you." I answered my friend. She kept at me – I had sold over one hundred fifty tickets, over ten times as many as anyone else, and she was dying to know my secret. I kept insisting she wouldn't believe my answer, but finally gave in:

I had taken sticky notes, written Nutcracker Tickets on a bunch of them, then stuck them everywhere – the refrigerator (of course), my lingerie drawer, on my dashboard, on the bathroom mirror – anywhere they would be visible all the time. That's it!

I was right. She didn't believe me. "No, but how did you DO it???" "That is how I did it!!!" This was the truth. The visual was the key. I knew that "if I built it, they would come". All I had to do was write and post the notes!

"But, did you..." "Cathy, I just posted the notes!" I insisted again. You may be thinking like my friend. I MUST have done something else.

I had just finished reading "The Magic of Believing" at the time and this was one of the simple techniques suggested in the book for achieving what you want. My friend wasn't sure she approved of this method. She didn't think it went along with Christian teaching. But I contend that the Bible teaches this principle in Proverbs 23: 7 NKJV, "As a man thinks in his heart, so is he." Any book you find on success and achieving your goals says guess what: write them down. It all begins as a thought, an idea in your mind. But when you write it down, when you visualize it, it becomes real. The psychological distinction is huge.

Why is this so powerful? When you see something constantly, when you are reminded of it as you go about your day it is almost impossible not to achieve it. If you ever lose your focus, you will get it back right away. But how does this work? As they say in Shakespeare In Love, I don't know. It's a mystery! You don't need to know why it works. I even hesitate to analyze it this far. The magic is in the mystery.

This technique has worked wonders in helping me in the trip-winning department. For my upcoming incentive trip, Costa Rica, I ordered two travel posters on Amazon – one with a Toucan on it, the other with a tropical beach scene – before the qualification period began. These went up right away where they would be seen in the house all the time. I also printed out the trip promo poster from my company to take with me in my car. This would be with me on my long-distance business trips, which were many.

The visual is crucial. For our small Christmas meeting with our business group, we decided to paint wine glasses at the local clay crafting place. Mine would say Costa Rica on it, and with my limited art skills, I would even paint the island itself, with the sea surrounding it. The glass turned out beautiful and was set out in our living room. Although the trip is already earned, the glass is still on display.

I wrote out Costa Rica in strategic places and proceeded to get busy planting seeds for my success the month before the contest began so that in January, the stage would be set to hit the ground running with a full calendar.

My method was the same as with the Nutcracker tickets. Once I put it out there, it would happen – regardless of any doubts or setbacks which might arise along the way. Doubts and setbacks are a part of life! They don't need to stop you.

On YouTube, the company's video advertising the trip was posted to watch – showing the gorgeous scenery, the luxury resort, and the consultants dancing the night away (not me, I would be the one up early, of course, but that's ok.) I watched it over and over, seeing myself on that fabulous beach and in the fancy pool. Looking for bathing suits was next!

I proceeded to collect travel brochures for Costa Rica, told people about my goal, and blocked out the trip dates on my calendar – this was a done deal! I completed the qualifications 3 weeks before the quarter ended. The winners were announced on one of the company's weekly broadcasts, along with our photos against a tropical backdrop. Costa Rica, here I come!

Don't underestimate the power of the visual. You can even do this on the cheap. As with the

Nutcracker tickets, use a sticky note pad! But do splurge on a travel guide to wherever you are going – one with lots of photos is best for your visual technique. Browse your guidebook before bed. Peruse it. Get it into your head. Plan your excursions and where you will shop. Your brain will be working on your goal while you sleep! Go on Amazon and get a jigsaw puzzle of your destination to work on with your family in your spare time.

"But how did you DO it???" Your friends may ask later. Now you have your answer: The Nutcracker Method!

EVELYN

You are kind, you are powerful, you are strong. ~ Adrian Williams, Peloton Instructor

We have to go back to my first company to meet a wonderful woman from my team there named Evelyn. She was already a businesswoman when she signed up with me, owning a quirky and gorgeous antique and collectibles store in the small mountain town near where we lived on the Air Force base. Signing Evelyn was exciting. She had the maturity and business sense that many new representatives did not and I was looking forward to working with her. But I soon noticed a problem.

Evelyn had decided soon after joining that she wanted to be on stage at her very first convention, and she was determined. The dominant type, no one could tell Evelyn anything. I noticed that she was ordering large amounts to meet her goal of getting on stage for sales, but she was doing absolutely zero appointments and wasn't selling her stock. I could always count on her if I ran out of something and needed it in a pinch – she had everything! I had to talk to Evelyn. As her leader, it was my responsibility and she was getting herself into trouble. Her husband was not happy about this state of affairs either, and I didn't blame him.

Trying to nip it in the bud, I encouraged Evelyn to do shows and sell. She would have been wonderful if she did! She was Miss Personality! I counseled her about stopping all the ordering until she was selling. We were in a cosmetics company and you didn't want products sitting around and going past their expiration. She wouldn't listen. All she could see was getting on stage, and that ordering was the way to do it. Since my efforts were ineffective, I went to my leader for advice. In the end, there was nothing we could do. In direct sales, it is your own business. Your leader can advise, but you are the boss.

Convention time came around, and Evelyn was on stage. No matter how she had accomplished it, I couldn't help but be proud of her. She was my only team member in that company who ever made it to the stage. Recognition can be a huge motivator, just like a trip, but if you put the cart before the horse, or eliminate the horse altogether, it defeats the purpose. These rewards are supposed to be the results of your hard work – not something you buy.

I lost track of Evelyn. Unsurprisingly, she didn't continue the business for long after Convention, and we soon were transferred across the country. I heard that she and Bob moved out of state also. I was out of direct sales during my years with the airlines, but there was no forgetting

Evelyn. When I found my current company and wanted to build a team, I spoke of Evelyn as a warning and asked my girls to consult with me on their ordering when they were new to avoid stockpiling and getting into trouble financially.

Evelyn is an example of what NOT to do. I guess if you are a millionaire and want to buy an incentive trip with a company, you could. But deep down you know you didn't earn it. And you miss out on the great sense of accomplishment and satisfaction you have when you are rewarded for really earning something the right way – with hard work and consistent effort. Don't take shortcuts. You will regret it down the line.

CHANNELING

Learn, relearn, and outlearn.
~ **Lailah Gifty Akita**

You don't have to be perfect to win an incentive trip. You don't even have to be "the best", whatever you think that is! You do have to want it bad enough and be willing to learn and get help. If you are unteachable, uncoachable, stubborn, and determined to go it alone, you may still achieve the trip, but you are hurting your chances and making the process needlessly hard on yourself.

Find those who are strong in your weak areas and learn from them. Nobody has it all. Even the top person in your company has a lot to learn. I was fortunate enough to meet Deborah about halfway through my journey with my current company. I could tell early on that Deborah had what I did not. I admired her confidence, but there was something intangible about her, something I found it hard to put my finger on. I noticed that things that might bother me, distract me, and get me off track didn't seem to faze Deborah. Sometimes these distractions held me back. That was a problem – one with which I still struggle and one that Deborah didn't have. Sometimes I allowed my feelings to overcomplicate things. Deborah kept it simple. The best in the business do! Deborah became my example.

We all have the same bumps along the direct sales road. Those who succeed have good shock absorbers. Deborah didn't waste time dwelling. She got on with it. Although kind, she also didn't put up with foolishness. I was guilty of spending too long on prospects or clients who were draining my energy and should be cut loose. Not Deborah. My husband's favorite saying is, Nice doesn't kill Migs. Nice is great – but you can be too nice and get taken advantage of. Sometimes letting someone go is the best option. Their time may come later.

Elaine, my roommate on the Cancun incentive trip, had it all going on. Yes, she was younger and more energetic, but again there was the confidence factor and the intangible piece. I had always been plagued by self-doubt and inadequacy feelings. Elaine and Deborah didn't have such tendencies and it showed. Working at a well-known bridal salon when she began with our company, Elaine had done two parties, quit the salon, and never looked back. Fear and laziness were not in her vocabulary. I left Cancun resolved to not only be more like Elaine but to find others just like her for my team! In the years since we met, I have seen her skyrocket to company fame!

Jenny was already my favorite trainer when the company CEO assigned me to her roundtable group at National Training. As she explained her methods, I was impressed, but argued, "I am not like you. I don't have your personality." To which Jenny gave a quick comeback, "If I give you a thousand dollars, can you fake it?" Well, when you put it that way. When did I need to "fake it"? Since chemo, I got tired more easily, but I realized I could be an actress! I could fake it when needed. I could "Be Jenny" at least temporarily and salvage the moment. It was like channeling. When necessary, I could let Jenny sort of take over my body. Whatever works! She didn't even know I was "channeling" her. It just became a mental trick that worked wonders for me.

You know those bracelets that people wear, WWJD? I began to ask myself, what would Jenny do? Then I would become Jenny for a few minutes to get the job done! Jenny's training that day made a difference for me in a way that no other training had. On a tough day (notice I didn't say a bad day! Tough days can be good too!) I learned to ask myself if I give you a thousand dollars, can you fake it? Sometimes, the reward amounted to much more than a thousand dollars! Although I had already won many trips by the time I was in Jenny's class, she helped me take my game to a new level.

Perhaps these three stand-outs could inspire you as well. But my weaknesses may not be yours. Take an honest look at what habits, tendencies or thought patterns might be holding you back in your business. What may have to go in for you to reach the trip goal? You can find those answers, and you are the only one who can. In my case, I benefitted from the example of others. I also learned to get out of my own way. It is something I still work on, winning trips along the way! In your imperfection, you can win trips!

HOSTESS COACHING AND APPOINTMENT PREP

Traveling for me puts things into perspective. It allows me to realize that there are far bigger things than my problems. ~ Anna Faustino, Adventure in You travel blog

This subject is so important that a whole book about it is included in the resources section. So much fantastic training on this subject is already out there, that I almost skipped this chapter! Then I realized that some of you hadn't had the opportunity to take advantage of that training just yet, plus I had a few nuggets to add of my own that will compliment any training you have already had. So here goes!

Now that you have done all this work to get your parties or appointments, how do you make sure they hold? That's where coaching and party planning come in.

Every hostess or client is different. Some are worth their weight in gold. They are dependable, invite plenty of people, are excited, and get others excited. They love your product, whatever it is, and are ahead of you every step of the way. I have several current hostesses who fit the description. For them I am grateful. Hostesses like this are also rare. On the opposite end of the spectrum are the clients who never respond to you and keep you guessing. They may ghost you. They don't invite people to their Facebook event and you have no idea if the party is even going to take place. I've got a couple like this right now too. Fortunately, most hostesses aren't like this either. Most are somewhere in between. Wherever they fall on our hostess meter, coaching is vital.

If your cancellation rate is concerning you, take a look at your coaching. Have you fallen down on the job? Have you kept in touch with your hostess as well as you should? Just like the Magic Five when it came to getting appointments, the Golden Three below will keep you on track with making sure your appointments hold – and are successful.

The Golden Three Steps are: Devour all the training you can find on coaching your hostess or client, Keep in close touch with your hostess, and make your hostess feel special. Just like we did with the numbers in the beginning, we are going to break down these steps to make sure nothing falls through the cracks. If you think you know it all about hostess coaching, bear with me. You just may learn something new.

1. Devour the training – Even experienced consultants need to be reminded of how important hostess

coaching is to their business. I wondered if focusing on hostess coaching was getting too far away from the focus of trip winning. Then I realized that this is EXACTLY where it should be. But it isn't enough. Make sure first that you have fully taken advantage of any training your own company has on working with your hostess. Then look further. Information is everywhere. (You can begin with the resources section just a few pages away.) Then search YouTube and Facebook for further tips and tricks. You can learn so much from other representatives and business people outside of the usual official channels. Put these tips to work, and see your cancellation level go down and your success go up.

2. Keep in Close Touch - When you first schedule your appointment, ask the hostess what the best way is to reach her. I have even been known to ask, "You aren't one of those who never replies, are you?" A friendly smile is on my face, but I'm serious. I address this when we first schedule her date so she knows we need to keep in contact.

Fortunately keeping in touch is now easier than ever. Some hostesses are Facebook message queens – they are super easy to reach this way. Use Facebook messages and voice clips. Use the Facebook event itself too. I coach hostesses to like my posts and comment on them to get the engagement and activity going on the event and to tag certain guests if they think a post applies to them.

As soon as you create the Facebook event, private message the link to your hostess and tell her it is all ready for her to invite. If a day or two passes and you can see the hostess hasn't accepted as co-host or invited anyone this is not a good sign. Follow up by text, voice clip, or phone call to make sure she saw it. If she is going to flake out, you want to know now so you can free up the date for someone else and not waste your time.

After a few days with no action, contact a mutual acquaintance if you have one and ask whether she knows if her friend still plans on hosting her party. Ask if she is ok? She may have had an emergency or problem arise that has become a priority for her. If you still do not hear back, reach out again and let her know that you will free up her date unless you hear from her! Keep it light. Don't burn your bridges. A better time may come for her.

I have had hostesses who ghosted me contact me over a year or so later, saying now is a good time. I'll take it! Always stay in touch and stay on good terms. I may contact her in a month or two and say I have had a date open up that is a prime date, and I thought of her. It is worth a try.

Always do a "day before the party call" to make sure no last-minute snags have come up for her.

Ask if there is anything you can do for her before the party. If she has had difficulty, see if you can help. Doublecheck on the time and see if she thinks the guests will be ready to begin then, or should you give it a few more minutes? You would rather know ahead of time that 6:15 or 6:30 is more realistic than 6:00. If your guests will all be seated and ready to go at six – you want to be prepared for that too! Just like when preparing for your trip, anything you can do ahead of time to make the party run more smoothly only benefits you.

Let her know when you are on your way to the party, and make sure she gives you directions to her home. GPS is nice, but not always reliable. If her's is a large apartment complex, get the name of the complex as well as the address and ask her for directions once inside.

3. Make Her Feel Special – My hostesses receive a packet in the mail created just for them. I purposely do not give it out in person. I want that extra contact with her. Most of us don't receive special mail very often. Getting something nice in the mail is a real treat! I include a small gift and handwritten thank you note BEFORE the party, thanking her for scheduling with me, along with samples, catalogs, and a sponsoring brochure. If you read the Partnering with Your Hostess book suggested in the resources, you may decide to meet for coffee and give her this in person. (Make

sure you pay for the coffee!) I highly recommend this book. All kinds of wonderful ideas for creating a real relationship with your hostess are inside! Since many of my hostesses are long-distance, I often have to use the mail. But whichever way you do it, the packet is such an important step in solidifying the hostess's partnership with you.

Any time she follows through and does what she is supposed to do, give her feedback. "Nice job inviting!" "Hey, Nancy, I just noticed you invited forty-three ladies! That is so awesome! I can tell already this will be a fun group. I can't wait for your party." Messages, texts, and voice clips all work.

Perhaps your company has a Hostess Bingo or a similar motivating game you can send her to play. Each square is something else she can do for her party. Then the stage is set to contact her again – "I think you have a really good chance for line five! All you need now is two pre-orders for your party to complete that line!" Keep her engaged and give her ways to earn more hostess benefits such as free or discounted products.

Some business trainings tell you to make sure and not cross the line into friendship with a client, but I don't pay attention. I make friends with my hostesses all the time and some have become truly close. I make a special effort to comment on posts about her children or reaching her fitness goal rather than just "liking". I also might private message her should I be concerned, or if I see she is having a special occasion. It takes time, but it is a worthwhile investment in your clientele and besides, she might need you. Maybe you will be the only one who bothers to message!

Keeping the Golden 3 in mind will take you a long way towards making sure your appointments hold and are successful. If a cancellation does occur, perhaps that one was not meant to be. You can always try to book another hostess in her place, offering something extra special. If nothing works for that date, enjoy some family time or even time to yourself. Self-care is important even during trip winning time! Make sure and refill your tank.

LET'S PARTY!

It's showtime! ~ Beetlejuice

You've done the work to fill your calendar, you've coached your client, now it's time for your appointment! Here is where it all comes together. Whether it is a sponsoring interview, a home party, a house showing, or a one-on-one, this is where the rubber meets the road. A house showing is very different from a home sales party, but the principles are the same. Whether you are selling a home, cleaning products, a water-filtering system, or your opportunity, you are going to be genuine, caring, excited, and ready! No matter what your product, putting your whole heart and energy into the appointment is the key. If you have done your preparation work, this will be the fun part. Having a winning mindset going in is essential. First impressions going in make a big difference. You can't allow something to hold you back from being "all there". So let's look at how to make sure you are fully present in the moment.

Part of this is the discipline of the professional. She leaves her problems at the door and makes her client and guests the focus of her attention. She is having fun with them – it's not an act. Sure, sometimes she may need to "channel" herself through a challenging situation, but she can do that with grace and style. She can do it, and still, be herself. For my guys, sorry for the feminine pronouns, but please adapt it to you. You want your clients to know you are truly interested in them, and not just there to make a quick buck and leave. (Believe me, I've received complaints over the years about the other kind.)

In my company, we provide a private one-on-one shopping time. This is partly due to the nature of our product line, which includes intimacy and bedroom items. But a private time is important no matter what you are selling. Even if your products are health and weight loss supplements, that person may want to tell you something private enough that they don't want to say it in front of other guests. The same is true of cosmetics or any number of other products. I strongly recommend each client have a time when they can receive your full attention and in as private a setting as possible. During that time, it is all about them. See what will truly benefit them. It may not be your most expensive model or item. Upselling techniques are wonderful, but only if that upgrade truly benefits the person to whom you are selling. The same is true with a home, insurance, or anything else. If someone is drawn to my most expensive item, sure I'm excited! And I will be happy to sell it to them! But I won't try to talk someone into it who doesn't need it or will be happier with something else. If you always keep in mind what is best for the client, that will benefit you in the long run as well.

The same principle holds in sponsoring. We want them to sign up under us, especially if we are in a multi-level company. But has she been working with someone else all along, and you just happened to come along at the opportune moment? I always refer her back to that person at least once and ask her what her preference is. If she truly prefers to sign with you, that's one thing. But how we treat other business people matters. Do the right thing.

ALONG THE WAY

It's the Climb. ~ Miley Cyrus

During your journey, you will have many days when you are excited, focused, in the zone. Things will be going your way. Those are wonderful days. Enjoy them fully. You will also have other days. Times of doubt may arise – doubt in yourself and doubt about if you have selected the right goal. Those days are a normal part of reaching for the big prize. Everyone has them. But when you get one, you can feel alone.

Times like this come not only when working for a trip, but also when trying to lose weight, or when writing a book, or trying to complete a project! You can get bogged down in the process and lose your joy.

On those days, take a step back. Take a breath. You will get your mojo back but get in touch with what is going on right now. Do you need a break? Do you need a day off? Or do you need to take action? Do you need to go through this alone? Or would connecting with someone be better?

Be quiet, and let the answer reveal itself. Take your time. This all comes down to awareness.

At some point when working for each incentive trip, an awful moment came when I thought, oh no. I don't think I'm going to get it. Maybe these thoughts were triggered by the cancellation of an important appointment – they probably were. But things will not all go smoothly at all times during your trip journey, and this will affect your mood and thinking. In each case with me, the moment passed, and I was able to take a deep breath and go forward with confidence. You will too. One cancellation does not a failure make. You should have enough appointments to allow for cancellations and no-shows anyway.

If you doubt, reread a section of this book that has been particularly helpful or inspiring for you. Go run around the block, or even just walk. Fresh air is underrated. So are endorphins – both will refresh your brain cells and lift your spirits. A big part of trip winning, maybe the main part, is in your head, in your belief. Your head will do better when you have fresh oxygen working in your bloodstream.

If you find yourself dreading an appointment or if your confidence flags, acknowledge the feelings, then go ahead to your appointment! As soon as you greet your client or hostess, and get your mind off yourself those emotions will dissipate.

Have some go-to affirmations you can use to get your mind back in the right space.

Try these:

God is with me.

I've got this!

I like myself.

People are waiting to hear from me today.

I am here to be of service.

I am having the time of my life!

Self-talk can make or break you. You are in charge of your thoughts, so get them in gear. It may be time for an inspiring movie or even just one to take your mind off things so that you can get a better perspective. Some suggestions are listed in the references. Or pick your own!

Take away from this chapter the fact that you are not alone, you are experiencing normal feelings and thoughts, and you can do something about them! Pick even one of the suggestions above, and make a start.

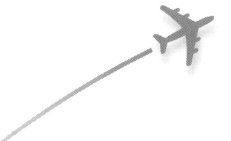

FAILURE FACTORS

Work, Travel, Save, Repeat. ~ Anonymous

What might keep you from winning a trip? Good intentions and even hard work are not enough for what you are wanting to accomplish. Several things can work against you. If you avoid them, you have a much better chance not only of achieving your trip but having a better time along the way. These are not the only things that can hold you back, but they are my top four.

1. Bad Attitude
2. Being Inauthentic
3. Distractions
4. Being in the wrong company

1. Attitude If I had to pick the most important factor in your success for trip winning – or anything else – it would be your attitude. Your state of mind. With the right mindset, you can accomplish almost anything. Occasional doubt or discouragement is normal, but allowing it to set in can be a killer. You will lose your mojo and mojo can be hard to get

back. Sometimes negativity just becomes a bad habit.

One person I knew in the business was doing amazing in both sales and sponsoring. Unfortunately, a negative mindset held her back from achieving even more, causing her to move on to a series of other companies. Here is a newsflash: you will not ever find the perfect company, or church, or school, friend, or even mate. You just need to find one that is perfect for you and focus on the good points. The key is "for you". You don't have to like or agree with everything, but you need to like most things in the marketing plan, policies, and products. A company is like a big family. Families don't agree on everything either. It is normal to have different opinions. But do you find yourself often critical of your company or your leaders? Have you let a bad attitude creep in? We all need to vent occasionally, but is complaining a pattern for you? Is nothing ever good enough? Be honest with yourself.

Could you be a more positive person? You can change, and you will be much happier when you do! Take a look at the resource section of this book and make a selection from the reading list. Those books are there for a reason. If a setback or something upsetting happens, negative emotion is natural, but try giving yourself a time limit for letting it affect your mood. Do you need to text or call someone trusted to get it off your chest? (Sometimes this makes you feel worse, so honestly ask yourself what would help you in the situation.)

If something is no longer serving you or your business, perhaps a group or meeting of some kind, let it go. Your time is valuable, and time is money, so make sure you are spending yours on what is helpful.

Exercise, positive reading and movies, spending time with upbeat and successful people, accomplishing something (especially something you have been putting off), giving yourself fun rewards along the way – all these work wonders for keeping you positive. When you do feel down, don't compound it by beating yourself up. Just do your best to get back into that positive frame of mind, and later evaluate what caused the bad feelings in the first place so you can avoid it in the future.

Is something holding you back from feeling positive? Procrastination? Your weight? Your marriage? Your drinking? Your spending habits? Debt? A messy or disorganized home? A bad relationship? I'm stepping on dangerous ground. But did you just identify with one of these areas? Plenty of help is out there for any change you need to make. If something like this has been in your way, now would be a great time for a change. Again I refer you to the reading list. Start with The Four Agreements. I like this practical book for everyone because even a child can implement the simple ideas in it, and make some real improvements in their life.

Limit your time on social media. More dangerous ground! But you don't need the drama, the meanness, the negativity, the gossip.

Finally, find someone you can help! Nothing lifts your spirits like getting your mind off yourself and helping others. Even a small kindness, donation, or word can change the tone of your day. Practicing such things can change the tone of your life, and business.

Find the support you need, and take it one day at a time.

2. Being Inauthentic The cheerful woman introduced herself on the phone, "I think your business card is so cute!" she said. "I'm with XYZ company, but that's not why I'm calling. I'm putting together a glamour book featuring ladies from different companies and I'm having a photo night I'd like to invite you to. It isn't to do with XYZ." This sounded cool! A chance to network and have a free glamour photo taken and be included in the book would be great! I never got a "book".

When I got to the event, I could immediately see I'd been a sucker. Ladies from XYZ were walking around in their special company suits, and the signature facial and make-up trays were set out awaiting our arrival. This was to be a total XYZ night. As soon as we arrived we realized that the "glamour book" was a ruse to get us to attend. She did take our photos, but that's the last we heard of the glamour book. Such tactics don't make people want to buy from or sign up with you. Quite the opposite.

In this case, the company wasn't at fault. This was the consultant's own dishonest approach to get women to attend her events, made even worse by the fact that she presented herself as a strict Christian, adding hypocrisy into the mix. Presenting yourself as spiritual to win the trust of others, then being dishonest is one of the worst turn-offs. In my opinion, this is a form of taking God's name in vain. When you invite someone to something, they should know exactly what they are attending. If you feel you have to trick people into coming to an event or recruiting evening, maybe you should consider changing to a company where you don't feel you have to use such tactics.

One of my party hostesses brought ladies into another room during my shopping time, and tried to sell them her purses without telling me. I had wondered at the time why my sales weren't higher that night in this upscale, million-dollar home. She was sabotaging me in another room. I never would have known, but one of the guests told me the next day. Using another person to get the clients there because you know they will be interested in her products, then proceeding to try and capitalize on that consultant's party by selling your things is tacky, and not the way to win a trip. Get your own party – or join the company you know gets the people there!

Are you being sneaky or dishonest? As much as we applaud Tess's tactics to get ahead in "Working Girl", as one representative said to me, word gets around. Some companies commonly use such methods – inviting people to something but not telling them what the event is, saying one thing and doing another, or trying to inflate claims as to their product or opportunity. Steer clear! If you are embarrassed about your company, get into another company! Do people cringe when they hear your company's name because it has a reputation for being less than honest? If so, do you want to be part of it?

Are you misleading potential guests or prospects? This will come back to haunt you. People find out and though it may seem a small "white lie" to you, playing games like this hurts your credibility. When someone finds out they have been played, they don't appreciate it. You can make someone feel special and selected without lying to them. People succeed using tactics like this, but then again what is your definition of success? If you make money or win trips but also gain a bad reputation, is it worth it to you?

The behaviors described here are one of the things that give the direct sales industry a bad name. Deal honestly and with integrity with your clients and team members.

Be authentic. Be upfront. Be kind. Be genuine. Doing so will serve you well as you pursue your dreams, and you will be able to go to bed at night with a clear conscience. Perhaps Mark Twain said it best. **"If you tell the truth, you don't have to remember anything."**

Distractions

They come in many forms, and they happen to everyone. They can be as seemingly innocent as your favorite Words with Friends opponent challenging you to a game, to more serious issues. Problems with kids, health and money problems, or a friend or client being difficult. Some representatives are thrown off track by the smallest daily irritants, others will not be derailed by anything. I have seen my company's founder deal with everything above, and not let it stop her. (Well, I don't know about the WWF...) These things will affect you, but they don't need to keep you from achieving your goal.

In my twenty-plus years in the direct sales industry, I've paid close attention to how the big shots have handled illness, personal tragedy, loss, divorce, and other huge difficulties. They have amazed me with their resilience, strength, humanity, and ability to bounce back. From my founder and CEO of my company to my sponsor, and other major players in the direct sales industry, they have not allowed these circumstances to keep them from their goals and dreams. They have fully felt them, wrestled with them, and dealt with them as best as they knew how and got help and support when needed. Then, they got on with it. One of their secrets? The same secret as my coach gave me as an assignment: find someone else to help. Although I don't know them all well, I do know some intimately and have marveled at this ability and strength of character to meet adversity head-on and find a way over, under, around, or through.

You can do it too. Remember, not all distractions are earthshaking. Some are small, petty, daily things that can make an impact on your mood and progress if you let them. How do I know? I've been there. Many times. Part of writing this book is seeing who I can help – even those I'll never meet. How about you? Who can you help today? You may be surprised at what comes your way as a result. Bought anyone a cup of coffee lately? You may entertain an angel unaware.

Sometimes beating distractions is as easy as disciplining yourself to keep going. Try one of my favorites: The Power of One. I don't know if he thought of it, but our CEO loves to give us this assignment. The best solutions are often the simplest: when you have finished what you are doing, do one more thing. In the sales room – sell one more item. When making calls, make one more. When you think you have completed an assignment, do one more thing to make it better. Do one more jumping jack! We can all do one more. I used this principle in writing this book, and I use it in my household chores, my business, and my errands. It is simple and it works! You will get more done, and if you make it a habit, you will beat your distractions and win your trip! It is all about what you do consistently, day to day.

Being in the Wrong Company

Lucinda was a winning package of personality, punch, and appearance. She loved being the center of attention and could have gone far with our company. One day I found out why she didn't. Lucinda was in a party company, and didn't want to party! She wasn't on my team, but she took a shine to me and liked working with me. One day she messaged me on Facebook wondering how she could get a refund on her World Conference registration (you can't) because she couldn't afford to attend. Knowing that you can easily make enough to cover your transportation and hotel in a couple of parties, I probed to find out the reason for her lack of funds. Come to find out, she felt home parties were beneath her. She liked our products but didn't want to be classified as a party person. I had to tell Lucinda that I could see why she didn't have the money for Conference! She asked why. Because you are not partying!

True you can do well with website sales with us as well, but we are very much a party company – both virtual and in person. We are designed that way and for a reason. Our products sell best when we connect with people. I hated to see Lucinda go, but she continued to resist doing party appointments, and eventually, she allowed herself to go inactive with our company and moved on.

If you don't like the platform or marketing plan of a certain company, winning a trip or advancing with them is going to be difficult. You have a real strike against you. Reread the chapter on choosing the best company for you, and see if another company is a better fit for you before you go for a goal as big as a trip. If you like where you are, fully embrace their way of doing business and go for it with them! But don't hold yourself back and frustrate yourself if you are in the wrong place.

MY ULTIMATE - DISNEY WORLD

Here you leave today and **enter
the world of yesterday**, tomorrow,
and fantasy. ~ Walt Disney

The photo of Mickey Mouse in front of Cinderella's Castle inside our company's annual incentive brochure had me at hello. Say Disney to me, and that is all you need to say. We could bring along three family members on this trip, and being a grandma that made it even more appealing! We would stay at the Animal Kingdom Lodge, all expenses paid. The requirements were higher than anything I had attempted yet. We had a choice this time of Disney World for 4 or Hawaii for 2. For me the choice was easy.

We had all year to meet the trip requirements, and as many as qualified could attend. A strong start right out of the gate was my style, and my January ROCKED. At one party, five ladies signed up as consultants. thirty people were at the party, and I had starter kits available for them in addition to a full stock of products, so they were able to take advantage of that, and they did! January turned out to be a booming start to the year, then came Valentines! Since mine was a romance company, this was our big season. I partied every night!

That year had it's lean times as well. I wasn't able to complete the full requirements until right at the deadline, but the trip of a lifetime was now only a few months away. The year had been productive and successful, and as my granddaughter ran up to me at the airport in Denver and we embarked on our Disney World adventure, I was so glad I had made the extra effort.

The Disney trip had required us to do $90, 000 in retail sales. Not every company wants you to keep inventory on hand, but If your's does I encourage you to do so. This was a huge factor for me being able to sell as much as I did, and I saved time that would have been spent packing and mailing or delivering. Keeping stock on hand, and having a back stock, is a great business strategy with lots of companies. You can take advantage of the impulse buy, and your customers will love taking things home right from the party. Just be careful not to overdo it, especially if you are new to the industry. If you are regularly holding appointments and making sales, in other words moving your stock out, regularly ordering makes sense. Your company may have inventory management training. If not, perhaps your sponsor does. Order smart as you work for your trip. You don't want to end up with a trip, but lots of credit card debt.

On the other hand, ordering more conservatively could cost more in gas and postage when you go to deliver or mail it later. Ordering ahead and having stock on hand is good business as long as you are consistently selling it. When I decided to take my business to the full-time level, I placed a large order so I could have a full stock of products, making sure to pay it off the same month. As long as you pay off your order within one or two months, that is smart ordering. Investing in your business is beneficial. Stockpiling, getting into debt, and letting inventory sit around getting old is not. Some consultants let their excitement to earn a trip cause them to do something they'll regret later.

Disney World turned out to be my best trip yet, for all kinds of reasons. But unknown to me, I was about to meet the biggest obstacle yet - to my business and my life.

THE ALASKA CRUISE

Perhaps he knew, as I did not, that the Earth
was made round so that we would not see too
far down the road. ~ Isak Dinesen, Out of Africa

I had the trip thing wired and had just started working for
the Alaska cruise when I got my first routine screening
colonoscopy. I had put it off for several good reasons: I
was a healthy vegetarian without symptoms, I didn't have
time, and most of all, my friend had died after HER routine
screening. The doctor had punctured her colon and killed
her. I wanted no part of that test. But during my annual
check-up, my doctor insisted and I figured getting it out
of the way was a good idea. The results would be clear,
the square would be filled, and I would never have to get
the test again! Well…not so fast.

The test itself was easy – the prep is not. The prep is
what makes everyone procrastinate about getting a
colonoscopy. Not only do you have to fast for a whole day,
you also must drink the yucky laxative drink they provide.
Fortunately, they also allow you to drink wine the night

before – white, of course. No red or purple foods allowed, or much food at all. But I could have my white wine!!! Thank goodness. After several trips to the bathroom, most test-preppers give up, take their phone, hopefully with Netflix on it, and stay there.

The test was a snap. But while I was lying in the recovery cubicle, my doctor came in with a grim look on her face – and a photo. You get a photo of your complete colon in full color, but mine wasn't a good one. Stage 3 cancer was present. I could see for myself.

After you hear the "C" word, your life is turned upside down. Surgeries, additional tests, and appointments are scheduled. You don't feel you have much say in the matter. I had a sense of losing control over my life. My head was spinning as I watched my life as I knew it, and my business, change overnight. I was to spend the next seven months in surgeries, chemo, and other treatments. So much for the other "C" word - the cruise. I hadn't given up on winning a trip before. It was not a good feeling, and this feeling was jumbled in with all the others I was trying to process on short notice.

Right now, survival had to be the top priority. The odds they gave me were not good. But surviving and losing my business for which I had put in so much effort over the years wasn't an appealing prospect either. Doing my best was all I could do. The Alaska cruise was not meant to be. I still hope to win it someday. Back then I had my hands full just doing the bare minimum in calls and appointments. Not being a "minimum" type of person, this didn't sit well with me. But I found that one of the effects chemotherapy had on me was mental. It made me not care. I just wanted to lay on the couch and watch tv. I tried to be in denial and act business as usual, but chemo was affecting my performance big time.

My kind of chemo required a device called a port to be installed in my chest (another surgical procedure), so that you could wear a "kangaroo pouch" around for 2 weeks a month, receiving steady doses of the drugs into your system. When you are getting chemo, and are on medications to counteract nausea and other side effects, you don't feel like doing much. Although everyone's cancer journey is different, most who have been through it will probably identify with this.

But I loved doing my parties. So most of the time my husband drove me and carried in all my supplies. The ladies were completely understanding about my having to sit down for my presentation. With those adjustments, and also cutting down on my number of appointments, I was able to continue my business, but at nowhere near a trip-winning level.

Partway through the chemo journey, when yet another new side effect appeared, I had had enough. Making a decision, I got home from the hospital and immediately went online to research alternatives to chemotherapy. Unfortunately, the laws in the U.S. severely limited choice in cancer treatment. But I found clinics in both Mexico and Arizona that sounded good. Selecting the Arizona one, I was on a flight the next day. I called from Arizona and left a message for my oncologist that I had flown the coop. I was quitting chemo.

The treatments in Arizona were given the same way as chemo – intravenously through my port. The only drug was DMSO. My particular cocktail contained mainly high-dose vitamin C, along with the DMSO (which stinks and makes YOU stink afterward), and other nutrients. Vitamin C oxygenates and alkalizes the blood, making it a bad environment for cancer cells. They had gotten all the cancer in the colon in surgery. That part had been successful. The idea now was to catch and kill any stray cells which had spread to the lymph nodes and might be hanging around waiting to cause mischief.

I took three treatments a week for three months, staying at my brother's house near the clinic. Getting my business going in Arizona during this time had very limited results. By the time my treatments were over and the dust had settled, I found myself back home in Colorado with no appointments and very little income. I had survived, but cancer had devastated my business.

Not having the energy to start over, but knowing this is what I wanted to do, made the journey forward tough. I was almost starting from scratch, and my usual methods for getting appointments weren't working. I was striking out. This had not been my year.

At this point, I contacted the company through the president's assistant to request a scholarship to their coaching program. He approved a three-month scholarship. I went into my first session thinking – ok, you have ten minutes to fix this! But during the coaching conversation, I realized it wasn't that simple. I wanted an instant formula, maybe like you did when you picked up this book. But there was more to it than that. My coach ended the first session with one assignment, "Go see how many people you can help today."

It wasn't what I had anticipated, but felt right to me, and I was willing to try anything. I don't remember who the first person was who I called, just to see what I could do for them, not to make an appointment or ask for an order. But I do remember that as my focus shifted to helping others, a wonderful thing happened. My phone started to ring. I had hit bottom and was on my way back up again. It would be a long climb, made harder by the fact that a post-treatment depression had set in. It was insidious, hard to recognize at first. I thought I was just having a hard time getting things going again. My enemy was invisible. Months would pass before I even admitted to myself what the problem was. Pride, denial, and unawareness kept me from recognizing and dealing with the depression.

A descendant of Swedish immigrants who made their own way, went through Ellis Island, and came across the prairie in a covered wagon, I thought the answer was to soldier on. I still think that was an important aspect of getting through what I was facing. But without coming to grips with the deeper issues, it would always be partly a façade. People were amazed at my cheerfulness, but much of the time I was putting on a brave front.

Lucy was right in A Charlie Brown Christmas. Recognizing you have a problem is the first step towards healing. Healing is a process. Not always an easy or pleasant one, but full of much enlightenment and punctuated rarely by crystalline moments of great grace, self-discovery, and incredible surprise. Just maybe, another trip was still out there for me. We would have to see...

JESUS AT THE BURGER KING

Fascinating. ~ Mr. Spock

During my Arizona treatments, a most unexpected moment of astonishment and blessing came my way in a very unlikely place. The Burger King in Holbrook, Arizona. During my three months of naturopathic cancer treatment in Tempe, Arizona, I was occasionally able to make the trek back home to Colorado to see my husband and spend a few days. My desert encounter occurred after one of these visits, on my journey back to my next treatment. I may have missed the Alaska Cruise, but something else was in store for me.

I never drove back in one day. I always made a stop in either Moab or Holbrook, depending on my route. This time Holbrook was the choice. But perhaps He would have appeared anywhere. The Croissanwich being one of my favorites, the Burger King was my first stop that day. A native gentleman, I guessed Navajo, was standing at the entrance talking on his cell, in workman's clothing, and holding a helmet. "No, it just won't start." He was saying,

I presumed to a boss or foreman on the job for which he was late.

He was still there when I came out with my little bag and asked me for fifty cents to get a cup of coffee. "Well, I'll buy you a cup of coffee!" I said. "Come on!" We went inside and I ordered him one at the window. The manager behind the counter didn't seem too happy – like he thought I had been taken by one of the regular panhandlers. I didn't care. We got the coffee and went back outside.

The man thanked me, and I walked to my car. But I couldn't get over the feeling that this wasn't over. I needed something from him too. Was this cancer treatment craziness? Would he think I was a nut? I decided if there was a time to throw caution to the winds, this was it. At this point in the treatment process, I was feeling desperate. I pulled up by the entrance, where he was still hanging out.

I got out of the car and walked back up to him. "Would you do something for me?" I asked. I'll never forget the way he looked into my eyes, deeply it seemed. "Sure." He said. "Would you pray for me?" There was no hesitation, no discomfort, no pretense. "Sure." He answered.

We proceeded to walk to my car together, and he put one hand on my car and took my hand with the other. He closed his eyes and began the most beautiful prayer in Navajo. As he spoke, and we held hands, I began to cry. I couldn't control it and who cared. I was in the moment.

Other customers were around. Who cared. My crying didn't seem to bother him. I had never heard anything so beautiful.

When he was done, he opened his eyes and looked at me. "You're going to be fine." He said. "I prayed for you, I prayed for your car, I prayed to the four directions. You're going to be fine." Still crying, I thanked him. I think we hugged. I can't remember clearly. As I got back into my car to leave, it began to occur to me that maybe he was an angel. Then I realized that I thought he resembled Jesus. As I drove out of the parking lot, the revelation hit me. He hadn't been an angel. Jesus had come to me at the Burger King in Holbrook, Arizona, and asked me for a cup of coffee. The Bible says that things like this happen. I had always envied those I knew who claimed to have seen Jesus or an angel with their own eyes. Now, I didn't have to. Maybe no one would believe me. I didn't care. I cried all the way to Flagstaff.

MIAMI BEACH SPA

Things could change. Things could
go your way if you hold on for one
more day. ~ Wilson Phillips

Soon after my desert miracle, my angel also appeared.
For the first time, our annual convention was not in my
budget. I never missed going, but serious illness often
wreaks as much havoc with finances as it does with your
health. When talking to my sponsor BJ on the phone one
day about my convention dilemma she offered to cover
all of my expenses completely – gas and hotel were what I
needed. My husband was attending this year too. BJ gave
me a credit card without any hesitation. I was speechless.
Overwhelmed by this kindness. She had put no conditions
on the gift (when BJ gives, she just gives without thinking
of the return) but I wanted to be worthy of it. I wanted
her to be proud of me and to start living my dream again.
With blessings like this, maybe I could make a comeback.

When I first joined the company, the Miami Beach Spa trip
to the famous Fountainblue Hotel, was calling my name.

As a new consultant, I felt the requirements put it out of my league. Many years would pass before that particular trip was offered again. When it was, it was the year after my cancer journey. The year after BJ's fabulous gift of the convention. Time for a fresh start and the perfect trip to inspire me to achieve again. I jumped in.

When we earned an incentive trip, the president of the company called to notify and congratulate us. We all looked forward to the prestigious call. For the Miami Beach trip, the requirements were such that even if you met them, you wouldn't know you were in the winning group until you received this call. The announcement went out when the calls would be made. The day came and went – no call.

I went to a meeting that night that a friend of mine was leading, and told myself that it wasn't the end of the world. There would be other trips. For some reason, though, I had a suspicion I might still get a call. I did. The next day after my husband left for the market, the phone rang (I had a landline phone at the time.) It was the president congratulating me on earning Miami Spa.

Another trip of a lifetime, another lifelong friend made with my roommate Sheri, great memories, and fun – but more than that, this time I had needed to prove to myself that I could still do it, that I wasn't a has-been. Miami did that – and what a town!! Many more trips were also on the horizon. I didn't know it then, but so was a book!

If your trip has requirements like this one, where you don't know until the end if you are in the "Top Five" or "Top Fifty", set the bar artificially higher for yourself so that you improve your chances. I preferred requirements like those on the Disney World trip, if I make the numbers, I get it! But not every trip is like that. Although it can be nerve-wracking as the end of the qualification period draws near and you wonder exactly where you stand, don't hesitate to work for a trip, no matter what kind of hoops you must jump through and what uncertainty you might have to face as you wait to be notified. Go for it! Don't hesitate. Make up your mind that you are the one to beat the odds. Setting the intention is the most important step – everything else comes as a result.

SPONSORING

Listen more than you talk.
~ President's Club member, Pure Romance

Often one of the requirements for earning a trip, bringing others into the business, often known as recruiting or sponsoring, is also one of the most fun and rewarding aspects of a direct sales business. Introducing others to your unique opportunity and helping them succeed along with you is exciting and fulfilling.

When working for a trip, you need numbers and you need them fast – so always have your antennae up. You never know who might be interested and you can't afford to overlook a key prospect. They may not jump right out at you, so be inquisitive, and listen. Find out what she wants out of your opportunity – no wrong answer exists.

Some leaders advocate screening your prospects and being selective, others advise you to take everyone. I fall into the second category. If you are "being selective" then you are making a pre-judgment on that person and her abilities. You could be completely off-base. Give everyone a chance.

When I finally decided to take my business seriously, I wondered why I was having so much trouble sponsoring. Why weren't women flocking to my company? I was a true believer, but for some reason, I wasn't attracting others to my team. My sales were good, and the party guests seemed to like me – so why wasn't anyone joining? I wasn't doing anything "wrong", but I could be doing better.

In the years since then, and many, many trips later, I found some tips that worked for me, and my sponsoring got into gear.

1. Be a good listener – If she is looking to make money, she may not be interested in how many friends she will make or how many trips she can win. Break down some numbers for her, and show her how much she can make and in what amount of time. If, however, she is looking to get out and meet more people and have some fun, you can focus on those aspects of the business. Say, "So talk to me – why XYZ Company? What is attracting you?" And listen to what she has to say.
2. Bring the kit with you!!! If your company requires the purchase of a starter kit, and you can bring it with you to the appointment or party, do so! If she can get it right then, that is huge to a lot of prospects. Don't let the moment pass – grab it! I jokingly say

at my parties that after my presentation, we are going straight into the New Consultant Training! I am only partly joking. Go to your appointment as much to sponsor as to sell. I have sold up to five starter kits in one party.

3. Be a "Recruiter" – live and breathe your company and opportunity! Be so enthusiastic that your opportunity spills out of you.

4. Numbers – Perhaps you are doing the first three, you just need to be talking to more people. The more you talk to, the more you can add to your team. This is where all those appointments we have booked come in. I believe new team members are at each of them – they may just not know it yet, and you may not recognize them, so be aware of who is there. I have added a new person when I least expected it.

5. Be a Good Sport – Not everyone will sign with you. When I find out someone signed with another representative or a different company my heart sinks a little. I wish them well and keep the lines of communication open. I may even buy from them! I have had ladies come back to me later. But if not, maybe the other company or sponsor is better for them. At least I like to look at it that way.

6. Follow up – When there is a special kit sale, or some big incentive is coming up, check with her again. It took me months to sign, others take years. See if it is her time.

THE BAHAMAS CRUISE – MAKING IT MEANINGFUL

My favorite place is somewhere I've never been. ~ Angelina Jolie

It wasn't until working for my tenth incentive trip that the idea to pray for my roommate during the qualification period came to me. This trip, the Bahamas cruise, was for consultants only, and a roommate, a fellow trip earner, would be assigned to us a couple of weeks before the trip began. I found it exciting, fun, and inspirational to pray for this person I'd never met and didn't even know who she was. Getting my focus off myself was also therapeutic.

Each time I had been assigned a roommate for a trip, we had become instant friends. The company president took it upon himself to handpick the roommate assignments, and I marveled at how well he seemed to know us. We always kept in touch after the trip and often became lifelong friends. My trip roommate became a go-to person for business answers, advice, ideas, and support. She would sometimes outperform me in her sales, recruiting, and advancement, so there was so much to learn from her. Sometimes it was the other way around. Some of my colleagues have told me they don't want to go on a "roommate" trip. They are missing out!

We always are so impatient to find out who our roommate will be! My company is worldwide, and for the Bahamas trip the roommate Chris selected for me was from Australia. June was even a grandma, like me! Shortly after we were notified of our roommate's identity, June decided to give me a video call from Australia, with her husband and whole family present! This was all the more special because I knew (she didn't yet) that this was the person for whom I had been praying for several months.

Did we ever have fun together! Shopping, eating, going to shows on the ship, all the things you like to do on a cruise. Our body clocks were opposite, so she might even arrive back at our cabin just as I was getting ready to leave in the morning, but we still got in lots of time. We both had a carefree approach to this incredible experience, made many new friends, and enjoyed rooming together during the whirlwind that was the Bahamas incentive trip.

So many fabulous excursions were offered! It was hard to choose. Because of my strong beliefs against dolphin captivity, I wouldn't participate in the popular "Dolphin Encounter", even though I would have loved interacting with these incredible creatures. My favorite excursion, horseback riding, was not offered on this trip. But we could swim with the pigs! These happy, friendly animals were born on a private, wild island and enjoyed growing up freely as they roamed to their heart's content. June and I both decided to swim with the pigs, although we ended up in different groups. Even during the instruction time with our Bahamian guides on the dock, the baby pigs mingled or rested among us as they wished, not seeming to mind that we were in their territory. When it was time to head into the water we were given pieces of apple on a stick, which the pigs loved to eat. The tide was low, so we weren't actually swimming, but we waded with the funny, sweet animals as they pointed their snouts up to the sky and opened their mouths widely, signaling that they were ready for their next apple tidbit. June gave me a mini rubber pig squeeze toy to immortalize the occasion. When you squeeze it, it oinks! The pig sits on display in my office, along with my other treasures I have gathered from my free travels!

June is back in Australia now, and I am in New Mexico. I keep track of her through Facebook and hope to see her again one day. As I write this, my eleventh incentive trip is approaching. Who will be my roommate this time? Whoever she is, I prayed for her too. I prayed for help with whatever struggle she might be facing during her trip-winning journey, for her breakthroughs, for great successes along the way. Adding this practice has made the whole process of working for a trip more meaningful for me.

But what if you aren't a pray-er? Find another way to help someone else who is working for a trip. You probably know someone, or could reach out on social media or through friends and find someone. Be creative. Encouraging someone else – by fun little instant messages, sending something in the mail, or an occasional phone call – will be a real blessing to them. But the secret is, you will probably get even more out of it. As in other aspects of a network marketing business, helping others succeed is what brings the heart into it, and makes it not just all about you. When you add this piece on your journey to the travel fairy tale, you will discover a lightness in your spirit and even a sense of relief as you get your mind off of yourself. Let God take care of you as you make the effort to help someone else. This will add a new dimension for you, and you can look forward to celebrating her success as well as your own!

What other ideas might add depth and meaning to your trip-earning process? You may already be giving a portion of what you earn away, to whatever person, organization, church, or charity that you value. If not, try it. You can't give away without receiving yourself. Send that money out to do good.

Try praying for the workers at the resort or on the cruise ship where you will be staying – for blessing, for their good health, and their spiritual needs. After our Bahamas trip, that wonderful collection of islands was struck by a catastrophic hurricane. I found myself remembering all the wonderful people I had met in the marketplace, or on the private island we visited, and wondering how they were doing. And what about the pigs? Were they going to survive? Praying was a way to reach out across all the miles.

Find your way. Be generous in your prayers and giving. I'd love to hear about how you have found ways to move forward with these ideas, and ideas of your own.

YOUR TRIP – TIME FOR ACTION!

To making it count! ~ Rose, Titanic

So who is ready to hit the dance floor? If you read this far, YOU are!

With this book, the end is the beginning! In my new consultant training, I tell my team members that when we finish our three-step training they will be ready to do their first party! They may not FEEL ready, but they ARE ready. After reading this book, YOU are ready to embark on your first (or twentyth!) trip earning adventure! You do not have to know it all to succeed. You just need to be inspired enough to get started and use the steps outlined in this book. Showing up is where it's at, as we used to say in the sixties.

Check out the resources section. You will find enough support there that you could do this on your own without any other help. They are that good.

Be too busy for the negativity going on around you. Don't be content to take the crumbs that fall from the direct marketing table. Ninety percent of representatives only scratch the surface and never get the goodies. They are cheating themselves. You must desire a trip or you wouldn't be reading this book – so it's time to jump in! Both feet, going for your dream. I can't wait to hear about the incentive trip you are about to win, the experiences you will have, and friends you will make. My vision is to do a second book containing all your wonderful trip stories and all you have learned!

If you take even half of the tips in this book to heart and work them consistently then you can be on that trip. The sales lifestyle is wonderful, but it isn't easy. What makes the journey worth it is all the rewards available to you along the way. The trips are the best reward ever.

THE PRAYER CONNECTION

"You haven't lost a hand since you got the
deal. What's the secret of your success?"
"Prayer." Butch Cassidy and the Sundance Kid

If you want my secret weapon, this is it. I pray hard all
through trip qualification time! I wouldn't know how to
reach any goal without it. Prayer is very personal, and we
all have our personal way of doing it – or not doing it. I
won't say you have to pray or be a certain religion to earn
a trip incentive. But you are missing out without prayer.

Prayer isn't always easy. Many books are written just on
the subject of prayer. But I'll take a stab at introducing you
to my style of prayer. I talk to God in my usual voice, in my
head, in silence much of the time. You don't have to do
the thee's and thou's. Nothing is wrong with traditional
prayerful wording, but I feel phony using it. I talk to God
as a friend or father, and I don't mince words. On a good
day, ideas will come to me during the prayer process, and
I take them as my answer. I keep it simple. Wherever you
are in prayer, don't complicate it. Begin with gratitude,

then stay there awhile. We would all benefit from dwelling in a state of gratitude more. During gratitude prayer and meditation, you may find yourself recalling someone who needs prayer. This is when I often think of those on Facebook, for example, who I said I'd pray for and may have forgotten. Now is a good time to catch up.

What does all this have to do with winning a trip? I'm not exactly sure how it works, but practicing gratefulness and realizing all the blessings I already have before making requests feels good to me. You don't have to fully analyze it. You can pray without having all the answers.

If prayer is not your thing, you may be tempted to tune out now. Stick with me a little longer. You have nothing to lose.

Adding visualization can be helpful in addition to just putting your thoughts into words. Let God know everything you want – including your dream to be on that ship or beach, or in that theme park. Reread my Nutcracker chapter. This all works together.

For me, everything flows from here. These are my best secrets. Prayer has been an integral part of my trip winning and every other goal I've achieved – and those I didn't. I couldn't do without it, nor would I want to. I need all the help I can get.

If you are new to prayer, try these easy ways to get started. In one of the books in the resources section, The Four Agreements, and its sequel, The Mastery of Love, prayers are included. Start there. Then you don't have to worry about what to say. Written-down prayers are underrated. Whole books of written prayers are available, or try some from the internet. You can graduate to prayers of your own as you feel more comfortable.

God knows your heart, but He still wants to hear from you. Not ready for prayer at all? Start with a guided meditation. Peloton Studios has wonderful ones on gratitude, kindness, courage, and even sleep.

A very special prayer in Navajo was a highlight of my prayer life. I hope you will be surprised in your prayer journey also. I admit that some of my prayers have been of the why-me variety, particularly during cancer treatment. Some were in tears. But as Mother Teresa says in my favorite quote, "Pray anyway." Start your prayer journey.

RESOURCES FOR SUPPORT AND STUDY

<u>Scriptures</u>

Proverbs 24:10, ESV "If you faint in the day
of adversity, your strength is small."

Proverbs 23: 7, NKJV "As he thinks in his heart, so is he."

John 14:14, ESV "If you ask Me anything
in My name, I will do it."

Matthew 6:6-8, NIV "But when you pray, go
into your room, close the door and pray to your
Father, who is unseen. Then your Father, who
sees what is done in secret, will reward you."

<u>Reading List</u>

Continue your study for success and inspiration
with these wonderful titles. Get them in
audio too for listening as you drive!

Be A Recruiting Superstar by Mary Christensen

The Four Agreements by Miguel Ruiz

Partnering with Your Hostess by Steve Wiltshire

How to Win Friends and Influence
People by Andrew Carnegie

The Magic of Believing by Claude Bristol

Knockout by Suzanne Somers

Health Resource

Nature Works Best Cancer Clinic

1250 E. Baseline Rd., Suite 205

Tempe, AZ 85283

480-839-2800

Movies for Business and Inspiration

"Moneyball" – Go ahead and think outside the box.

"Working Girl" – Let the river run.

"The Big Year" – Humor, heart, fun...and competition!

"Field of Dreams" – Create something totally illogical!

"All the President's Men" – Try this one after
you think you've had too many "no's"

"Chariots of Fire" – Dare to dream.

"The Cove" – about Dolphins. Please watch.

JUMPSTART YOUR TRIP!

Jill's 3-session Jump-Start Coaching Program
will start you off strong on your trip goal!

3 Sessions for a total of $99

This personalizes your trip journey for
the specific requirements for your trip,
and maps out your game plan!

These are private one-on-one phone sessions with
the opportunity to join with other representatives
in a group session at no charge. You also become
part of my private Facebook travel group!

Just Text your name and "I'm In" to
720-883-2209 to get started!

You can also reach me at this number to arrange
trip training for your team or company.

ACKNOWLEDGMENTS

Thank you to the training department at Pure Romance for all their fantastic resources and training opportunities. You have truly made it fun to "stay a student". You are a class act!

Thank you to Kristi McKibben for being an incredible hostess, customer, and friend over the years, and for providing me with insightful feedback on certain sections of this book.

Thank you to Bridget Dixson, Director of the Santa Fe Chamber of Commerce, for giving me feedback on the section on Chambers of Commerce, and the opportunity to be a radio show guest. It was fun!

Thank you to my brother, Dr. Scott Evans, for his encouragement in my writing process which helped me to become the 4th author in the family, and for letting me stay at his home during my Arizona treatments. That was beyond the call of duty.

Thank you to my CEO Chris Cicchinelli for picking only the best roommates for me on each trip! They have been the cream of the crop and become super great friends! Thank you also for offering inspirational and tempting trips every year that motivate us to work extra hard. And for my coaching scholarship.

Thank you to Mrs. Bahns, my twelfth grade English teacher at Oxnard High School, for teaching me how to write. I'm finally doing it.

Thank you Kris Hansen for giving me that party way back when, and being a mentor along the way.

Thank you to my beta reader, Baylei Renee, for taking the time to read my book critically. Since she liked it, you can blame her if you don't.

Thank you to my incentive trip roommates Amber Brarens, Sheri Vech, Valerie Spear, Elaine Eisinger, and my Aussie friend June Power! Rooming with each of you was a total pleasure and I treasure the memories with all of you. (I know the number of roommates does not match the number of trips, but not all the trips had roommates! Remember Disney World which included family!)

Thank you to Steve Wiltshire and his team for being an inspiration on both attitude and how to work hard as a direct seller, and how to do so with integrity, honesty and a sweet spirit. I appreciate your book and coaching program which helped me so much as a new consultant and as my business grew.

Thank you to my daughter Emily and granddaughter Sophi for listening to me read portions of this book, and giving me their opinions and loving criticism. I love you both so much.

Thank you, BJ Jones, for all the reasons I talk about in the book, but also for just being you and being the inspiration and example you are in the business. Thank you for the flowers too.

Thank you to Pure Romance for eleven fabulous incentive trips, and many more for which I paid with my Pure Romance earnings. With you I was able to make my travel dreams come true!

Thank you, Honey, for your belief in my writing, my business, and all my efforts. Your support makes all the difference.

Thank you, Jesus in the desert, that I am still here.

BONUS!! CREATE A TRAVELING LIFESTYLE

Don't quit your daydream. ~ Annonymous

Travel is my passion. Is it your's? You've gotten started on that incentive trip. Let's look at some other ways to get free, or close to free, travel with your business.

First, pick a trip! You will make more money and get to your goal more quickly when you are excited and specific. Saving the money you make at your parties or on your website or with your monthly bonuses without a definite goal in mind is great – but a little boring. Boring is not helpful. Where is your dream trip? Do you long to take the family to Disneyland, or on an Alaska cruise? Do you want to backpack through Europe for 2 weeks, or enjoy the theater district and historic sights in London? Is Fiji or Australia more your style? Or perhaps you are thinking of a singles or other theme cruise! Whatever travel excites and motivates you, that is the trip to pick! Even if you long for a visit back home, you need money.

Of course, you need to work your business and make money, and meet people to sign or get on your team, whether this is through parties, events, or mainly online. All methods work, and each business fits better with some than others. What is your strong suit? Capitalize on it – that is where you will make money easiest. It is fine to explore new options and ways to expand your business, but as I tell my team, the tried and true will work for you! Reinventing the wheel is usually not the best plan. Work with what you know, and be open to new ideas as well. Now, look at how you can put more money in your travel budget, even without increasing what you are already doing. You'll be on that beach or mountain peak in no time!

1. Have a credit card that gives you travel rewards or points that can be used for hotels and airline tickets. Some cards give you points with each purchase which can be cashed in for money to be spent any way you want. You can watch the points accumulate each month as you work for your goal. Use this card for your inventory orders if you keep stock, and the points add up quickly just for doing your business day to day. Have a goal for when your points reach a certain amount, say what you will need for lodging or your airfare. After a few months, you can estimate how long you will need for the points to add up to the amount you want. Other cards give you air miles as your rewards. As you watch your miles accumulate, you can begin to plan when to purchase your ticket. You

will be ordering a lot during your incentive trip qualification – use this card exclusively for your orders, and when you win your trip, you will have a significant amount of points for the trip of your choice too.

2. Set aside a certain percentage or amount from each appointment, order, party, or bonus. Do what works for you – Fifty dollars per party, one hundred dollars per bonus or override check, or ten percent of what you make total each week or month, or three hundred dollars per home sold – these will add up quickly.

3. Schedule your fun trip to coincide with a company event, such as a convention or training. This will make a portion of your trip tax-deductible. For example, if your convention is in Orlando or even Atlanta, you can plan on driving there, then going to Disneyworld or Universal before or after your event. Combining trips makes them much more affordable.

4. Make plans to drive, and do business appointments on the way to and from your destination. This may not work for London or Bali, but for many domestic destinations, it is quite feasible. When I won the Las Vegas trip, I drove and made a side trip to Disneyland, paying for my hotel with my credit card points. The trip was almost free!

5. Go in the offseason. This can save you hundreds, even thousands of dollars, and make a huge difference in your travel budget. Many places are seasonal, and the hotel and airfare prices reflect this. AVOID SPRING BREAK AND PEAK SEASONS IF AT ALL POSSIBLE and you can stretch your dollar.

6. The Bottle Method – this is a fun way to save for your trip. Rinse out your empty wine bottle and let it dry. This is now your collection receptacle for all your five-dollar bills! If you discipline yourself to put them all in your bottle, you will find your travel fund growing quickly. Are you planning a family trip? Have your family contribute their five-dollar bills as well! It is hard to get the bills out of the bottle so you won't be tempted. When it is time for your trip, you get to break the bottle!

Use these tips and you will end up earning many trips instead of just one!

EPILOGUE

A successful book is not made of what is in it, but of what is left out of it. ~ Mark Twain

My husband is an artist. Every time he almost finished a painting during our thirty six year marriage, he would want to start over. Whenever he said he was done for sure, he would drive me nuts by continuing to work on it for days, which turned into weeks. The painting looked great to me. Well now, I know how he feels. Each time I thought I was close to being done, another tidbit you just had to know would come to mind. A book is like a painting.

We can talk about the Dominican Republic, Las Vegas, Naples, and Chicago and other magical places another time. This is plenty to get you started and get you winning. My greatest thrill would be to see you do just that. Share your trip winning triumphs with me and on our travel Facebook group!

The parting words will not be from me, but fittingly from Royal Caribbean:

"GET OUT THERE!!!"

Printed in the United States
By Bookmasters